DR ANDREW WAKE is a child and adolescent psychiatrist with extensive experience in both public and private practice. He has worked in a range of settings, from leafy suburbs to rural townships and remote Aboriginal communities. He has lectured at the University of Melbourne, and also undertaken numerous speaking engagements at mental health clinics, schools and child protection units on topics such as parenting, child development, adolescent sexuality and the effects of childhood trauma. He lives in Melbourne with his wife and three children. This is his first book.

THE 'GOOD ENOUGH' PARENT

Designed and typeset by Caz Brown
Typeset in 11pt Sabon
Printed and bound in Australia by McPherson's Printing Group, Maryborough, Victoria

National Library of Australia
Cataloguing-in-Publication data:
Wake, Andrew P.
The 'good enough' parent: how to provide for your child's social and emotional development
ISBN 978 0 646 57404 2 (pbk)
Includes bibliographical references.
Parenting. Child development.
649.1

THE 'GOOD ENOUGH' PARENT

DR ANDREW WAKE

For children

CONTENTS

INTRODUCTION

A father I once met at a child's birthday party said to me, 'It's hard to know what to do sometimes; if only kids came with an instruction manual.' He was joking, of course, but after years working as a child and family psychiatrist, and my own experiences as a father of three, I realised how useful it would be if parents better understood the developmental influences on their children's behaviour, so I sat down to write this book.

This book is different to the many parenting books out there that attempt to teach you how to 'manage' your child, though this one still contains plenty of case studies and useful strategies. Instead, my aim is twofold; firstly, to help you understand how children's early experiences and their amazing brains work together to influence their social and emotional development, and secondly, to explain what you can do to provide what children need for healthy development.

The 'Good Enough' Parent is not meant to be a textbook of child and adolescent development, either. The theoretical ideas in it simply provide the background to the clinical work I do with parents, teachers, child protection workers and others who have children in their care. Although written with parents in mind, it would be a useful resource for any person who works with children.

The way I see it, when it comes to your child, you and your partner are the experts. *You* know their temperament, their character, the resources your family has, and so on. I'm not here to tell you how to raise your child, but to give you the background knowledge that will allow *you* to devise strategies that will work for you. This is important, because there is nothing like parenting to make us doubt that we are 'good enough'.

Every day I see parents crippled by self-doubt: 'Am I doing the right thing?' 'Is it my fault that he's like this?' 'Please tell me what to do.' Confidence is important when we are responsible for children. Most of us can more or less change nappies, make dinners, clean the house, and sing nursery rhymes – providing for a child's physical and intellectual needs is the easy part – but juggling their social and emotional needs (along with our own) is the great challenge. Yet, as with our children, our confidence can only grow if we are responsible for making decisions, taking risks and putting in the hard work to make them happen. This book is the first step to developing your confidence.

In Part 1, I explore child development from the point of view of attachment (the mother–infant bond) and its effects on your child's emotions, behaviour and relationships. In many ways, this is our children's core need: to get enough of us. But this 'getting enough' must be balanced with its opposite: 'missing out enough'. Although children need to be securely with us, they also need to separate from us, and in Chapter 2 I explain how important it is for parents to allow their children to miss out – how, in some ways, parenting can be considered the 'gradual disappointment of children'. I then consider the loss and grief associated with children's perception that they are missing out, and their rage at unmet expectations.

In Part 2, I look at what we can do as parents to support the development of our children's emotional understanding and regulation, and their skills for healthy relating to others. As adults, we know too well that learning involves trial and error, and very often the discomfort of failure. Children will always experience suffering as they develop (some more than others) and it is difficult to watch this. Some parents find it harder than others to see their children fail, lose, miss out or be left out – particularly if they have unresolved, painful experiences from their own childhood. But if we protect children from the suffering that comes with growing up, we stunt their growth and may even give them the unconscious message that we don't think they can cope. We need to understand them, provide for them, support them and believe in them; but we cannot grow up *for* them.

My aim is to help you see yourself as a 'good enough' parent, rather than tie yourself in knots trying to be a 'super' parent. From this confidence will flow strategies that will best help your children grow into strong, calm and connected young men and women.

Of course, understanding what to do is important, but the *really* hard bit is the doing. It takes bravery and courage to change. It may be encouraging to know that many have gone before you (including the writer), and you are not alone in desiring change in your family's life. And when you find it difficult, know too that you are not alone. I have had the privilege of witnessing and participating in many parents' struggles and successes as they seek to help their children, and I wish to acknowledge the inspiration they have been to me. I wish you all the best as you work towards supporting your child to become the best person they can be.

Andrew Wake
March, 2012

Note: Families come in many configurations, though for the sake of brevity, I've written this book as if each child has two biological parents of different gender. Whether you are a single parent, a relative who is effectively a parental figure, a permanent carer, a partner of a biological parent, or an adoptive parent, you are an important attachment and therefore parental figure to your child.

Also, the case studies in this book are not individual ones disguised with a name change – they are 'compilations' based on the numerous children and families I have seen over the past twelve years.

PART 1

WHAT YOU NEED TO KNOW

CHAPTER 1

ATTACHMENT: GETTING ENOUGH

Around 200 million years ago, reptiles were among the most advanced animals on earth, and humans were nowhere to be seen. Reptile brains were relatively simple, and had perfected all the bits and pieces necessary for survival. There was no need for language, planning, wondering, or any of the other remarkable cognitive skills we humans have, so their brains were also quite small.

Then something remarkable happened. One of our reptile ancestors began to develop a new part of their brain that improved the chances of their offspring developing into an adult. No longer did the young animal basically have to fend for itself after hatching. Instead, this new brain area was responsible for a stronger relationship between a mother and its baby – a bond that lasted much longer into the young animal's development. This enduring attachment between mother and baby was the beginning of the rise of mammals.

With these new capabilities the mother actively nurtured and protected her young, giving them a much greater chance of surviving those dangerous early years. This mammalian attachment between parent and offspring gave protection and closeness, nurturing and care, and guidance in learning about the world – advantages which, over millions of years, ensured that mammals became dominant throughout much of the earth.

About two million years ago, a new type of mammal evolved: the human. We still had the reptilian part of our brain – survival was still our first need – and we still had our mammalian brain – attachment (belonging, caring and being cared for) was still the next most important need. But our new human brain was massively expanding, literally filling up our head, and with it came our ability to think, plan, wonder, sing, talk and do all the other remarkable things that humans can do.

Yet, even as humans became smart and flexible and thoughtful, deep down the reptilian and mammalian parts of our brain were as influential as ever. Before we can think, we need to feel securely connected. And before we can feel securely connected, we need to feel safe. When it comes to your child, at times you will be parenting a thoughtful human, but at other times you will be parenting an insecure mammal or a frightened or enraged reptile. (See Chapter 3 for more on this.)

All children have a deep and overwhelming need to be attached, and attachment theory is an immensely helpful way of understanding how this need influences our child's emotions and behaviours. Attachment theory was first developed by John Bowlby in the 1950s and continues to be a major influence in our understanding of child development. It arose from observations that a child's early experiences seemed to be strongly associated with how they developed emotion regulation, how they related to others, and how they viewed themselves in the long term. It is now an enormous field, encompassing brain scanning, neurochemistry and evolutionary studies as well as classic longitudinal studies, and is getting bigger every year.

In explaining attachment theory to parents and clients, I summarise the following key points:

1. Our child's main motivation is to be safe. Nothing moves him like feeling unsafe, and all other needs are secondary. He must feel safe if he is to be able to adequately learn from and securely interact with others.
2. Our child's main way of experiencing safety is by feeling securely connected to her 'attachment object' – usually her mother – who soothes, protects and makes her feel safe and secure.

3 Our child responds to feeling insecure with 'attachment behaviours' (crying, smiling, talking etc.) so that he becomes reattached and feels secure. And he will do whatever it takes to feel this way.

These attachment drives and behaviours are deeply ingrained patterns that are a function of a child's specific temperament and experiences in the first three years of life (all prior to the development of logical thought). So when relating to others, children tend to follow well-worn patterns that have little to do with logic or reality, and can be very hard to change. This is why when you ask your child, 'Why did you do that?' you will often get the answer, 'I don't know' – because they genuinely *don't* know. What drove their emotional responses and behaviour came from their mammalian brain, a more unconscious part of their mind.

At times the adolescent clients I see will talk to me about their confusing, intense and mixed emotions: 'I don't know why I feel and behave the way I do. It doesn't make sense.' However, many of the parents I see also struggle with their own patterns of relating to others, which affects how they relate to their children. Logically they know they should try to be positive and supportive, but they may find themselves constantly criticising and seeing the negative in their children. 'Why do I do this? My kids are great, yet I keep jumping down their throats over little things.'

This is where understanding comes in. Your child may not understand their intense emotions, relationship patterns and behaviours, but you can. And your understanding can help your child understand themselves.

ATTACHMENT AND SAFETY

During the nine months of pregnancy, your child was literally attached to his mother. Her body provided everything he needed: he was never cold, hungry or alone, and suffered little discomfort. He was also constantly surrounded by the music of his mother's heartbeat and voice. This is one of the reasons why singing a lullaby and rhythmic movements such as rocking and walking (especially at 60 to 80 beats per minute, the mother's heart rate) is so soothing to our children when they get distressed; these hark back to that time of bliss. In fact, to the most ancient part of our brain, anything that mimics the womb can be experienced as very soothing (see 'Soothing the Reptilian Brain' on page 74).

When your child was born, this 'paradise' was lost: the continuous physical attachment ended and the constant music ceased. For the first time, your baby could feel hungry, tired, cold, lonely and in pain. Of course, he did not have words for his discomfort. All he knew was that he felt awful and he wanted that feeling to go away.

So what did your infant child do when he felt the discomfort of hunger or coldness that this separation had allowed? Did he solve his own problem and fix his own distress? Of course not; he cried. And in crying he was able to make his distress *your* problem. You responded to his cry by going to him, trying to work out what the problem was, and then doing something to soothe him. You didn't support him while he sorted his own problem out; you took on the responsibility for solving the problem and saved him from his distress.

This instinctive way of coping with discomfort is very powerful, and is a way of coping that never leaves your child. Though they get older and discover new and more mature ways of dealing with their difficulties, when they feel they cannot manage, and if their distress is high enough, their most basic and automatic way of coping is to do something to make their problem your problem so that you solve it and save them. This is quite understandable and helpful when your child is an infant, as they usually need to be saved; but as they grow it is much less helpful for them to continue to make you responsible for their problems, and to use you instead of themselves to solve their difficulties.

Michael's amazing mother

Michael was a nine-week-old baby who had woken from sleep and started to cry. It began as a mild fussy whine, but over two minutes it quickly turned into a roar (his mother, Kate, was having a shower).

'Not again! Can't I even have a shower in peace?' thought Kate. Though a bit annoyed, she quickly got herself ready and went to see Michael. Clearly the baby was not going to calm himself. Kate had to work out what the problem was and how to soothe him. Her first thought was that he must be hungry, but the cry sounded a bit different – more frantic, even angry.

By the time she entered the room she had gotten over her own annoyance at being dragged from the shower, and began to try to solve the puzzle. He wasn't cold, his nappy was dry, and when he saw her his cry stopped. 'Come on, you. I know what you need.'

Michael was picked up, kissed, playfully jiggled a bit and bounced slightly on the pillow while she got ready. Then Kate offered him the breast. Initially he was a bit frantic and sucked quickly, but he soon settled, and a rhythm was established as Kate patted him and hummed a tune. After ten minutes the sucking had stopped, and Michael looked up at Kate with an expression of contentment.

So within the space of a few minutes Michael went from whiny, distressed and angry to deeply contented and calm, and the difference was due to his becoming reattached to his mother.

Just like little Michael, your child experiences separation as being associated with discomfort; and reattaching as being associated with feeling soothed and safe.

The secure base: a place to reconnect and repair

So you are their secure base, a place they can always go to reconnect and repair, a place of certainty and bliss. As your child gets older, his development occurs as a series of journeys away from you (taking a risk) and back to you (returning to safety and security). Your child's task is to find the balance between taking increasing risks as he pushes the boundaries and develops mastery of new things, and returning to security to recharge his emotional battery. On returning he shares the excitement of his successes, or is comforted in his failures. Whether he succeeds or fails, is irrelevant – either way he knows he is okay and that he belongs. A problem may have occurred, a mistake made, but it is okay as it can always be repaired. This going away and coming back, making mistakes and experiencing repair, happens constantly throughout childhood, and it is the stuff of learning and growth. If your child never leaves, he may stay safe, but he learns nothing. If your child never makes a mistake, he may avoid the shame of failure, but he learns nothing.

The vast majority of learning comes not from being close and being perfect, but from when we return and mistakes are repaired. It is vital that we separate, and it is vital that we make mistakes. How terrible for your child if you never stuff up and never have to repair any disconnection with them. Fortunately, being perfect is impossible; but even the attempt to be perfect can be a problem.

The relationship between a parent and a child is a constant dance between togetherness and separation, abandonment and reuniting, mistakes and repair. With a thousand experiences of reuniting, your child learns that separating is not a threat; and with a thousand experiences of repair, your child learns there is no need to fear making mistakes.

Your task is to be aware of and support both your child's need to explore and master his environment, and his need to return for comfort and to make sense of the anxiety and excitement of his journey away. You must find the balance between letting him lead and letting him get lost; between anxiously holding him in, and prematurely pushing him out.

Insecurity

If security is that wonderful and comforting experience of being close and connected to your carer and protector, then insecurity is its opposite: the experience of feeling disconnected, overlooked or abandoned. Though insecurity *feels* bad, it is actually a good thing that your child can feel it. She needs to feel uncomfortable if she finds herself too far away from you and in a dangerous situation otherwise she won't be motivated to return to where it is safer – by your side.

From an evolutionary perspective, insecurity has been vital for our species' survival. Children in early hunter-gatherer tribes would have been surrounded by many life-threatening hazards, and their survival would have depended on adequate protection by the adults in their tribe. To be separated, abandoned or unattached would have meant death. Those who survived were 'programmed' to feel insecure when too far away from their parent or guardian. In other words, human beings have evolved to do *whatever it takes* to feel attached and secure. *Nothing* else is as important, and all else (including thinking, playing, exploring) will be sacrificed to attain this goal of safety.

Feeling secure = 'Can they see and reach me?'

Have you ever been at a park with a child who is about eighteen months old? Perhaps you were sitting on the rug and your child toddled away from you. Do you remember that at a very predictable distance your child would turn around and look to see whether you were watching her? If she was within a particular distance (inside the 'safety circle' which was unique for your child according to her temperament) she would continue her exploration and play. But if she found herself beyond a certain distance (outside the 'safety circle') or she thought you were not looking at her, couldn't see her, or were focusing on someone else, she would either do something to get your attention or would come running back to you.

The reason for such behaviour can be explained by attachment theory. In those early years, if she was within the circle of safety she felt secure: she could think, play and explore freely because if she got into trouble she could be reached. But when she found herself outside that circle her ability to think, play and explore was overridden by insecurity and the drive to get back 'across the line' where she believed she would be within reach and thus safe.

Feeling secure = 'Am I on their mind?'

As your child develops, and his journeys away become further and longer, his measure of security changes from physical distance ('Am I within their reach?') to psychological distance ('Am I on their mind?'). He feels okay if he believes that you are thinking of him and that you know where he is. In other words, he is certain that he has your attention.

'Attention-seeking' behaviour can thus be reframed as 'attachment-seeking' behaviour; driven by your child's wish to feel safe. This means your child can be standing right next to you, yet feel very insecure because he does not believe he is on your mind enough. Conversely, he can be many kilometres away, yet feel completely secure because he believes he is on your mind.

Note, however, that it is not whether you are *actually* thinking of him that matters, but whether your child *believes* you are. This is an important distinction to keep in mind. You may be thinking of him, yet he feels insecure because he believes you are not (or not thinking of him enough). Children who feel secure are actually on their parents' minds very little, but it is enough for them. In contrast, insecure children are often on their parents' minds five, ten, twenty times as much, but it is not enough. As one mother said, 'What does she want from me? She says I never think of what she wants, but all I ever do is think about her!'

The solution for a child's insecurity is not to think of him *more* (your role is simply to think of him enough), but to help your child develop the belief through experience that he gets enough of your attention and that he is on your mind enough.

The pain of insecurity

If you've ever wanted to be with someone and been ignored or rejected by that person then you know what it's like to feel insecure. Many popular stories feature main characters who have been abandoned or orphaned (think Oliver Twist, Harry Potter, Annie, and Frodo Baggins) because most of us strongly identify with the pain of loss.

Insecurity is experienced at an emotional level rather than a logical level (see Chapter 3), and these emotions can influence our children's thoughts and behaviours without them even being aware that they originate from insecurity. There are three broad groups of emotion associated with insecurity: sadness, worry and anger.

Sadness

For some children (and adults) insecurity manifests as feeling mildly upset or teary, while for others it develops into intense sadness and even depression. Sadness is sometimes less obvious in children who withdraw and are very quiet or 'shy', or who 'run' from their emotion through intense physical activity or obsessive pursuits.

Worry

This group of emotions includes unease, fear, trepidation, nervousness, self-doubt, anxiety and panic. Added to this are the physical symptoms anxiety can bring such as poor concentration, insomnia, appetite loss, fatigue and irritability. Worry is less obvious if expressed in actions such as avoidance, or in physical symptoms such as headaches or stomach-aches.

Anger

These emotions include frustration, hate and destructive rage (where a child wishes to hurt or punish). Sometimes this anger is directed at the people they love, and sometimes it is directed inwards. Anger is obvious when it is actively expressed through yelling, hitting or biting sarcasm ('By the way, you're the *worst* mother in the world!'). It is much less clear when expressed passively through whining, complaining or asking for help and then rejecting the help that is offered. (See Chapter 2 for more on anger.)

Some children seem to have predominantly angry reactions to their insecurity, but in my experience, behind this anger there is a hurt, sad and anxious child. In most anxious children there is often a thinly veiled rage directed at a parent for not being able to soothe their distress. And sad children may be grieving a loss, but are often also anxious about the possibility of further losses, and angry that the loss was allowed to occur in the first place.

Think about times that your own child has shown extremes of sadness, anger and worry. You will probably find that these arose when the child experienced difficulties in an important relationship. Whether your child's emotions seem to you to be reasonable or absurd is irrelevant – it is simply how they feel. In this context, emotions are neither good nor bad; they are simply telling us something.

Just as pain tells us that we are in danger of damaging our bodies:

- Sadness tells us that we have lost something important
- Worry tells us that danger is near
- Anger tells us that someone has disappointed us
- And all three are associated with the experience of insecurity.

ATTACHMENT BEHAVIOURS

So far I have tried to explain how our children *feel* when they are insecure. I want to turn now to what they do when they believe they are 'not on our minds'.

As we saw earlier, in the first months of infancy your baby's response to discomfort was to cry – one of the few ways she had to communicate. This resulted in you responding and your child feeling soothed. A cry can also be a complaint about not being soothed and being allowed to become upset in the first place – 'How could you let this happen to me?' And finally a cry can be demanding, in that your child only considers their own distress, and wants it solved immediately without any thought to others' needs.

It is very hard to ignore a crying baby. It is a piercing sound that elicits various mixed emotions. While you can decide not to *do* anything in response to a cry, you cannot stop the feelings you have when you hear one. Sometimes we may feel angry with ourselves for not being able to soothe our child. At other times we may feel angry with our child for demanding so much from us: 'What more do you want? Leave me alone!' The recent popularity of the tongue-in-cheek book for adults, *Go the F**k to Sleep* about a child who won't fall asleep is a case in point. It shows how we can become angry when our best efforts to help our child don't work – angry at them and angry at ourselves. The book also highlights the value of humour when trying to deal with these difficult and intense emotions.

At about six weeks, your child develops another important attachment and communication behaviour: smiling. Its purpose is to get you to interact with her. When your child smiles at you, you respond by smiling, laughing and talking to her, picking her up or playing with her. Like crying, smiling is also an effective attachment behaviour, but it has the added bonus of getting your child's attachment needs met without the corresponding negative emotions that crying and complaining can elicit. In fact, a child's smile is more like a request. She is not demanding your attention, but *asking* for it – asking you to interact with her so that you both have a lovely time together.

Crying and smiling can be considered the two archetypal attachment behaviour styles, and your child will use a mixture of both to get her attachment needs met. Most of us would prefer 'requesting smiles', but 'complaining cries' are always used to some extent as they are so much more effective. A child who is laughing, smiling or giggling is much easier to ignore than one who is crying or screaming, and when your child is feeling particularly insecure (unthought-of and disconnected), she is likely to use whatever works best.

'The smile' attachment behaviours

As your child develops, she gradually discovers more subtle and sophisticated ways to feel secure. Like the smile in infancy, these positive attachment behaviours are healthy and adaptive ways to feel connected. They include touching, talking, being helpful, humour (making people laugh) and sharing experiences.

Touching

Requesting a hug, a cuddle or a kiss; holding your hand; sitting on your lap and playing with your hair are all experiences that help your child feel secure. Whether initiated by your child or yourself, these experiences promote a strong sense of safety and connection. Though not literally touching, eye contact is considered to be a particularly powerful and intimate 'touch' attachment behaviour between parents and children.

When a child is feeling insecure, she can overdo 'touch' and come across as smothering, needy or clingy. This may lead the parent to push her away to get space, which unfortunately reinforces the child's insecurity and further increases her attempts to reattach with touch. This sets up a pattern that, instead of leading to loving connection, leads to disappointment and dread with the child feeling she never gets enough and the parent feeling the child's needs are insatiable.

Talking

When a child talks to us, and we truly listen to her, she *knows* she is on our mind. Yet as with touch, children who feel insecure can overdo talking to the point that we end up only 'half-listening', which leaves them feeling insecure again, and so the cycle continues. (See 'The Attachment Battery' on page 22 for ideas on helping your child to feel more secure.)

Being helpful

We all want to be thought of. We all want to be considered. We all want our needs to be recognised. If we are sitting alone crying and no one notices or responds, we feel disconnected and alone. If we are anxious about a coming event and someone notices and responds to our distress, we feel connected and comforted. It is why we intuitively understand that remembering birthdays and other events is important, and why when you meet another's need in an appropriate way it builds the relationship. Our actions are saying, 'I have noticed and responded to your need; you are on my mind.' In contrast, this need explains why being taken for granted is so toxic to relationships: 'You and your needs are not on my mind.'

Sharing humour and play

In my experience, families who get the most from family counselling are the ones for whom humour and playfulness are important. Shared play with your children is a deeply connecting experience. As a parent, sometimes you lead, sometimes you follow, and sometimes you are so in sync with your child that you seem to play together with the one mind.

A shared joke is one of the most potent experiences of attachment we can have, and is often a time we feel most connected to others. Stand-up comedians describe their success as euphoric and their failure as 'I'm dying out here.' Humour is usually subtle and people can only share your joke if they are thinking of you; if their mind is elsewhere they won't get the joke.

Of course, not all humour is positive. Sarcastic humour or put-downs, where people share a joke at the expense of another, are some of the most powerfully disconnecting experiences we can have. Telling 'in-jokes' can be a cruel way of defining membership of a group – determining who is in and who is out. Our adolescent children are particularly good at using in-jokes to help define group membership. If you cast your mind back to school days, you will remember times when you were 'in' and when you were 'out' of particular groups. Being the only one to not get the joke can be a painfully excluding experience. It is not hard to see that if you put your child down and shame them, whether in jest or not, you are setting up an unhelpful dynamic in which trust is replaced with anger (and with it, often the desire for revenge).

Sharing experiences

This may sound obvious, but as adults, the people you are most connected to are usually the people you have shared significant experiences with, such as studying, training, working or travelling. In the same way, the experiences we have with our children are crucial in building our connection with them. We need to share their triumphs and tragedies – watching them play sport, playing games with them, walking with them, holidaying with them – as well as the more ordinary daily tasks such as eating meals and doing chores. Each shared experience becomes an invisible thread connecting you and your child. And those memories of you can be taken with them, giving them a secure emotional connection to you even when you aren't within their reach.

'The cry' attachment behaviours

If the more subtle positive attachment behaviours fail to get their attachment needs met (them being on your mind), children will eventually move on to the more negative ones. As an example, a smile only works if the parent can see it and even then it can be ignored; a cry works even if the parent is next door, and can rarely be ignored. More demanding attachment behaviours are more effective in the short term, but generally result in immature coping strategies and less secure relationships in the long term.

Creating conflict

There is nothing like a fight to get someone to think about you. When two people are involved in active conflict, each person is on the other's mind to the exclusion of all else. However, once the fight is over, people feel even more insecure. I have seen many conflict-ridden families whose members find, perversely, that it is only through ongoing conflict that they feel connected.

The other 'benefit' of conflict is that it allows us to express the anger we feel about being forgotten or ignored. Anger is so effective at getting attention that it is no wonder many children learn to use it so early (think toddler tantrums) and to express it so easily.

Conflict with our children is inevitable given that we will undoubtedly disappoint them throughout their development. Our role as parents, then, is not to prevent them from becoming disappointed and angry (an impossibility because deep down what they want from us is everything), but to tolerate their attacks and help them learn how to express their anger in healthy ways. If our child exclaims by words or deeds, 'I hate you' or 'You're a bad parent', instead of reacting with our own rage, anxiety or defensiveness, we need to tolerate their disappointment in the confident knowledge that our child gets enough, and say in our words or actions, 'That's okay. You'll get over it.' See Chapter 2 for more about dealing with anger and disappointment.

Provoking by nagging or deceit

Like crying, nagging is hard to ignore. A nagging child is saying:

- 'I'm distressed and you don't care.'
- 'You are not giving me what I need.'
- 'I'm feeling hurt by what you are doing.'

Because we are anxious to protect our children, and our instinct is to keep them safe from harm, such accusations can be very confronting and we may either give in to their demands quickly (usually to avoid our own discomfort), or feel so irritated that we react negatively ('Will you give it a rest for a minute!'). Either reaction is not helpful in the long term.

When we react to their nagging and provocation, they have our attention briefly, but frustration is likely to increase in the long run. This is because snapping will feel like criticism, giving them the message that they are 'not okay'. Over the longer term this makes them feel more insecure, so they are more likely to keep on nagging.

Lying and deceiving are more complex provocations, and it is important we understand them so we can respond in the most helpful way. Broadly, there are two overlapping reasons that children will lie or deceive:

1. To get something they want that they know they can't have
2. To avoid the shame and embarrassment of not measuring up to someone else's expectations.

When children lie, try to remember that it is a universal experience that they are learning to deal with. Instead of lecturing them or feeling outraged, think of it as an opportunity for you to help them understand their desires for the things they can't always have, and their fear of being shamed for not measuring up (see 'Emotion Coaching' on page 31). But also remember that the lying needs to be talked about; if it is not discussed it cannot be repaired, as Jack's story illustrates. (See Chapter 4 for more on repair.)

Jack

Jack grew up in a family where few things got repaired. Whenever there was a disagreement or a fight, people got angry and walked off until they calmed down. They would then return, but the problem was never discussed – it was simply allowed to blow over. By way of example, Jack's father once criticised his wife in bed, and she told him to sleep in the spare room. Two months later he was still sleeping there. Then one night he simply came back to the bed, and everyone behaved as if nothing had happened. The initial problem was never spoken about or resolved.

Jack had a fear of making mistakes, as they would generally result in him being told off, after which there would be silence all around for hours or even days. Jack had no confidence that mistakes could be repaired, so he discovered early on to hide his mistakes by lying. He lied about big things, he lied about little things. And when he was caught for lying, he was roundly criticised and shamed, which reinforced his lying to avoid the shame. Telling Jack to stop lying and punishing him had no effect. Rather, it was only when his parents were able to sit down with him and talk about why he lied, how he could have managed the situation differently, and at the same time allowing the emotions that came up, that he was gradually able to stop lying and feel confident to make mistakes. In other words, his parents had to work on consistently and authentically repairing the relationship after he lied, instead of shaming him and sending him to his room.

Being helpless

This is where children demand help (and therefore your attention) to solve a problem. It is more than asking for assistance to deal with their own problem (which is known as 'affiliation' – a mature way of coping). Effectively they are making their problem your problem and demanding that you save them by solving it. It is the immature but powerful way of coping with distress discussed at the beginning of the chapter: when overwhelmed by something, they look to their protector to take the responsibility for the problem, and to soothe and save them.

Be very careful that you do not automatically rush in and take over. Even though you might think that this is 'helping' your child, and even satisfying his need for attention, in the long term it may reduce his problem-solving abilities and his resilience.

The best approach is to support your child as he works it out for himself, as this not only tells him that you believe he can work it out, but also gives him some practice at doing so. 'Saving' your child (telling him what to do or doing it for them) is important for safety reasons (if his life or health is in danger) or if his best efforts haven't been effective enough, but should be avoided as much as possible (see 'A Supportive Approach' in Chapter 4).

Some examples where children may try to get you to save them include the following:

- Completing physical tasks such as tying shoelaces, wiping bottoms, packing away toys or finishing homework ('I can't do it').
- Solving conflicts in relationships, especially with siblings ('Mum, Mary won't give me my ball back!').
- Avoiding situations or tasks they don't like by sensing your own vulnerabilities and drawing you in (e.g. if you were bullied at school, they might discover that describing their own peer problems at washing-up time gets them off the hook).
- Finding themselves in a dilemma and trying to get you to make a decision for them ('I don't know', 'I can't remember', 'Whatever you want', 'How could I know what to do?').

Being helpless is a very effective way to get us involved because we are strongly driven to help our children. It is not always straightforward when our children are suffering to find the balance between helping them and leaving them to help themselves.

Becoming Ill

There's nothing like sickness or injury to ramp up attachment between a parent and child. Most of us can't help showering an ill child with extra hugs and kisses and special treatment (food, staying home from school). No wonder children sometimes feign or exaggerate illness to get their needs met or to avoid responsibilities. (I once worked with a family that placed an excessive value on independence, and the only time physical affection was given was when someone was ill, so surprise-surprise there was a lot of illness in that family.)

If your child is genuinely ill, she will obviously need you to do things for her. However, if you are not sure whether the 'school day stomach-ache' is genuine it can be difficult to know what to do. If there are no physical signs of illness (temperature, rash etc.), it might be that something unpleasant has happened at school. Talking to your child (or another parent or teacher) is one way to find out if bullying is a problem (though don't ask your child leading questions such as, 'Are you being bullied?' Make them more general: 'Is there anything happening at school that is making you feel really angry or scared?'). Some parents find that if they give their child the benefit of the doubt and allow her to stay home but keep her confined to her bed for the day and don't allow her to watch TV or play any electronic games ('If you're sick, you won't feel like doing anything, so just rest, darling'), her ensuing boredom may ensure that she only wants to stay home when she is really sick.

Control

From birth, a human infant expects to have all his needs met, complains tremendously at any discomfort, and through attachment behaviours is able to control the parent to get his discomfort soothed. Being in control is thus associated with keeping the negative experiences of insecurity away; 'I get what I want when I want it.' However, as he grows, he realises that he cannot make his parent (attachment object) do whatever he wants – that there are boundaries and that some discomfort has to be tolerated. If these boundaries are repeatedly, predictably, firmly and kindly reinforced, they become a natural part of the child's life and perspective. Thus, the child learns that although he doesn't get *everything* he wants, he gets enough. With this he learns that not being in total control is okay, and he becomes stronger as he gradually experiences and tolerates increasing amounts of discomfort and suffering.

Children who don't believe they will get enough tend to retain their attempts to control: 'I'm only going to get my needs met if I'm in control of the other person.' This means that their relationships will be based on power and control rather than empathy, trust, and freedom. It is the difference between the belief that good things will be given, versus the belief that I will only get what I want if I take it or make it happen.

Avoiding attachment

If your child has tried a whole range of attachment behaviours, but still believes that she is not on your mind enough, the insecurity she feels becomes unbearable. If this happens, an alternative solution to deal with the insecurity is to try to convince herself that she doesn't care whether you are there for her or not. This is what may be happening when a child rejects what she clearly wants with statements such as, 'I don't care' or 'Whatever', and behaviours such as rejecting attempts to comfort or help her and even destroying the thing she wanted. She is trying to cope with her unmet attachment needs by denying or avoiding those needs.

Most people have experienced wanting a relationship with someone, but when it didn't work out, trying to convince themselves that they didn't care about that person. Often this is done by suddenly finding in the other person a long list of faults that had not been seen previously. 'If I don't desire the person, I can't be hurt by not having them.' This approach only works for as long as the desire can be kept out of awareness, and even then it only works partially.

David's story

David's parents had separated when he was fourteen. He lived with his father, and his mother had moved to another country to live with her new partner. Despite the distance, his parents' relationship was extremely toxic and David felt caught between them. He adamantly denied any problems with sadness, anger or worry (despite numerous home and school reports to the contrary) and struggled to even name emotions let alone talk about them. The only problem he could articulate was that he slept poorly and always felt tired. For two years he would cope for a while, but then explode mindlessly at his father after a phone call from his mother and then feel exhausted for a few days. He denied knowing why he got so angry, and denied caring about his parents' separation or not seeing his mother.

The explosions and fatigue only eased when he was able to acknowledge and talk about his grief, disappointment and anger at both his parents for not being able to 'get it together'. David's father could tolerate his son's attacks and was willing to put in the time to try to repair their relationship, so it gradually improved.

Unfortunately, David's mother could not change her pattern of becoming defensive whenever he brought up the separation and could not accept his disappointment, and the last I heard their relationship was still fraught.

The attachment battery

Attachment can be thought of as a form of energy that your child needs from you in order to grow and learn. When she is 'full' of attachment energy – feels secure and safe enough – she can play, have fun, think, take chances and explore the world around her. But when her attachment energy is low – when she believes she is not secure or safe enough – the drive to 'fill up' takes over, making it hard for her to play or even to think.

Young children cannot always be plugged directly into their attachment energy sources by being with you and obviously on your mind, so they carry inside them a 'battery' which stores attachment energy – they are in effect taking a bit of you with them as memories and experiences. With time the energy stored in the battery eventually runs down and your child is driven to return to recharge from you directly. Once their attachment battery is recharged enough, they are able to leave you again to play, think and try new things.

Other safe adults (such as teachers and relatives) can be temporary sources of attachment energy if a parent is not available, as can a phone call, email, photo or text, but if enough time passes even those alternative energy sources will not be enough to keep the battery levels up and the child will become increasingly focused on being with you again. If the battery level gets low enough leading to them feeling unthought-of and unsafe, a child will end up feeling seriously insecure, and high emotions and frantic attachment behaviours can ensue.

The 'recharging the attachment battery' analogy can help explain the commonly observed attachment behaviours of children when they reunite with their parents after a separation:

- **Touching.** They run to their parents for a kiss and a hug.
- **Talking.** They chatter away about their day and parents find themselves saying things like, 'I was thinking about you today' or, 'I was wondering how you went.' This gives them the clear message, 'You were on my mind even though you weren't with me.'
- **Sharing humour and experiences.** As parent and child think and talk about the day, there can be laughter as stories are shared and made sense of. There may also be tickling and playful touch.
- **Creating conflict.** They may pick on a sibling or do something that they know will annoy a parent to ensure they have their attention.
- **Provoking by nagging or deceit.** They may hassle the parent for something ('Can I have an ice cream?' or 'Can I go on the computer?').
- **Being helpless or ill.** They may talk about what went wrong, or show a wound to elicit sympathy.

If on seeing you again your child receives an insufficient attachment charge (because you are busy with other children, on the phone, or preoccupied with your own concerns) you would expect to see more emotions and behaviours associated with insecurity. Separating and reuniting are times when it pays to be aware of your child's attachment needs and to work on charging up your child's battery as much as possible.

Recharging your child's 'attachment battery'

If children are feeling insecure, have been away from you for a prolonged time, or are under more stress than usual, then touch, talking, humour and listening to their experiences are all positive ways of helping them to feel safe and secure again ('reattached' or 'recharged'). Every time you do this, they learn that not only will they get enough of what they need, but also that they can risk leaving you because they know from experience that you will be there when they come back, ready to support and soothe them.

To give children the greatest charge, practise the following:

- Stop whatever you are doing and focus on the child.
- Get down to their level so that you can make good eye contact. (Don't talk to them from another room and expect them to be happy with 'distant attention'.)
- Use some physical affection (a kiss, holding their hand, touching their shoulder, putting your arm around them, or cuddling).
- Reflect that you know they want your attention ('I know you'd really like me to spend some time with you right now').
- Briefly explain what you are doing, though this is less important than your gentle manner and kind tone of voice ('But I really need to finish cooking dinner').
- Give them a time limit for how long they have to wait for your full attention. It is best to start low and increase gradually using trial and error as a guide. And if you give a time, make sure you keep to it – broken promises are a sure-fire way of increasing uncertainty, disappointment and thus insecurity. If you do break a promise, don't beat yourself up (who can be perfect?) but simply apologise and tolerate their disappointment and anger, and make sure you don't break the next few promises if you want your child to believe that you can be trusted.
- Be confident about the separation and let them know that you believe they will be able to cope. ('I know you can do this. Remember yesterday how you went to kinder and I was waiting for you at pick-up time? Guess where I will be at pick-up time today?') And if your child is feeling a bit nervous about the separation, when pick-up time happens don't keep talking to the other parents, and definitely don't engage with the other children. Instead, focus on your child and charge up her batteries.

Doing these things regularly and predictably will help small children to feel more secure in their relationships. As our children get older they become more mature, but their underlying attachment needs still need to be met; the child inside of them that needs to be cared for, nurtured and protected never vanishes but simply gets its needs met in more mature ways. You might not approach an adolescent as you would a small child, but he still needs to know he is important to you and that he is on your mind.

ATTACHMENT AND EMOTIONS/RELATIONSHIPS

Have you ever noticed how fascinated teenagers are with mirrors? Often they will spend large amounts of time looking at themselves in various poses and with different facial expressions, and in various outfits. By looking at their reflection, they are trying to match what they see with how they feel – their outward appearance and their inner reality. It is a way of trying to work out, 'Who am I?', and 'Am I okay?'

Widespread access to mirrors dates back only a few hundred years so is a relatively new phenomenon in human history. Indeed, we evolved without being able to see what we actually looked like. We had to rely on others – their verbal and nonverbal responses to our appearance and behaviour – to find out whether we were 'okay'.

Our 'mirrors', therefore, were our attachment objects – the people who cared for and about us – usually our parents. Donald Winnicott said, 'the precursor of the mirror is the mother's face'. Our parents' responses to us were modified by their affection and love, and reflected more than our physical attributes. This 'modified reflective process' is an important way a child learns about themselves. When your child looks at you, they not only see you, but also a version of themselves in your response to them. Your child learns about relating with others and about themselves predominantly through the reciprocal relationship they have with you. Let's consider your mirroring role in the earliest months (how you respond to them and think about them) and how this helps your child's emotional and relational development.

The importance of mirroring

Weeks 1–4: Helping your baby be calm

At this age your task is simply to help your baby be calm, neither under- nor over-aroused. This means feeding her when she is hungry, changing her nappy when it is wet, and soothing her by cuddling, rocking or singing when she is distressed. Your baby needs to be calm if she is to learn to shift her attention from her internal state to the world around her (and so begin her amazing learning journey). *You* being calm in the face of her distress mirrors to her that her distress is not overwhelming and that it can be managed – that she will be okay.

How this influences later development

Throughout their development to adulthood, children frequently will be overwhelmed by their emotions and drives. In this unregulated state they are in no position to learn anything. By remaining calm, and gently but firmly containing her baby, the mother helps him gain emotional regulation. Being a calming influence and providing a calm environment is the first and most important step in helping your child learn about himself, whether he is two weeks, twelve months or sixteen years old. When helping them soothe themselves, what we do and how we do it (the approach) will be far more important than what we say (the content).

Weeks 4–8: Helping your baby pay attention

Your role at this next stage is to help your baby prolong her attention span so that she is ready to receive signals from you. Relaxed and playful looking into your baby's eyes is a particularly important experience for her from this point onwards. This intense gaze is hard-wired into a baby, and is not only a deeply connecting attachment experience, but also believed to be the beginning of the development of empathy in children. Talking and singing to your baby also help her to focus on your face. By doing this you are helping her to focus on you, her mirror, which is crucial if she is to learn about herself and others.

When eye contact is disrupted due to developmental problems in the child (such as autism spectrum disorders) or problems in the parents (such as post-natal depression, personality disorders, drug abuse) there is a much greater chance that children will develop emotional and social problems.

How this influences later development

As a child grows, many things will draw her attention (TV, computer, music, games, pets), and these distractions can result in poor focusing on important issues at hand such as handling difficult emotions or tensions within relationships. You may need to remove the distractions, and gently but firmly insist on your child's attention. This may require great patience on your part, but by showing persistence you are modelling that the emotional issue *can* be dealt with.

Weeks 8–12: Reflecting your baby's emotional state

Once your baby begins to smile, you will find yourself playing delightful games with him – he'll smile and coo, and you'll smile back and coo, and on you'll go. He'll not only *feel* the joy himself, but he'll see it on your face: your big smile, wide eyes and happy voice saying, 'Look at that big beautiful smile!'

Later, when he is crying from tiredness, you will mirror his frustration by scrunching up your face and speaking in a softer, more placating tone, 'Oh, dear. You're grumpy because you're tired. Let's get you tucked up in bed now.'

And when your child is frightened by a loud noise, your wide eyes and slightly startled expression will mirror in a modified and more bearable form his more intense distress, and you will give him a comment like, 'Oh, honey. You are a bit scared by that loud barky dog. It's okay.'

Being attuned to your baby's emotional state and reflecting it back to him is the beginning of helping him to be aware of and make sense of his own feelings. It is your attempt at understanding what is happening for your child – not making it about you, keeping your own issues out of it – and gently showing with facial expressions, gestures or words what might be happening for him.

How this influences later development

Almost all parents do this mirroring in the early weeks and months, but for many it starts to fade away in the toddler years as their child becomes more independent. These parents often stop wondering what is happening for their child and become preoccupied with their own role, their own emotions, or in finding solutions.

As an example, when your eight-year-old is distressed about not being invited to a friend's birthday, a mirroring/reflective approach would be to say, 'That's no good, honey. You seem to be a bit upset. It must be awful to feel left out.' A less reflective approach would be to say, 'Don't worry about her, she's not a nice friend', or 'Well, if you don't act in a friendly way, no one will invite you.' (The importance of reflecting is discussed in 'Attunement' on page 29, and also in Chapter 10.)

Weeks 12–16: 'Hatching' and your baby's initiative

At this time your baby begins to initiate interactions within you. This emerging independence has been called 'hatching' and is where babies begin to realise that they can influence their interactions with you. They may want more or less of something, refuse to feed or sleep, and they may complain more even though their needs are being met.

It is important that parents support this emerging desire for autonomy and freedom by reflecting their baby's initiative in a playful yet respectful way, and letting them lead where it is safe to do so. This allows the child to feel okay about their attempts to initiate, and encourages further attempts at exploring.

How this influences later development

If you don't wait for the child to take initiative, or override their attempts to take some control, the development of their autonomy can be impaired. The less reflective and patient a parent is, the more they will direct their child into what they want done, and the less they will allow their child to take the lead and learn for themselves.

When your child is a teenager, the drive to develop autonomy can become a mammoth issue and a source of much conflict and distress between you. As far as is safe and reasonable, supporting a young person's initiative is a vital part of building their self-esteem ('My ideas and wishes are good enough') and helping them develop the belief 'I can do this'.

Four months onwards

Emotions are central to relationships. When you are closely attuned to your child, she learns how to use subtle shifts in behaviour and emotions to regulate both herself and you in an appropriate and sensitive way. If you miss her subtle cues, she will use less subtle approaches to get on your mind. If eye contact doesn't work, then she might try a smile. If that doesn't work, she might reach out with her arms. And if that isn't enough, she might try a small whimper, then a cry, followed by a blood-curdling scream.

All this needs to be seen in the context of balance, however. The infant does not know what is and isn't reasonable when it comes to initiating, so of course she will sometimes fall short and at other times will go too far. Sometimes her initiative may need to be contained. From the age of four months onwards, your role is to work out what can be allowed and played with and what needs to be understood but limited – a task by turns joyful, infuriating and anxiety-provoking. And a task made easier if you are attuned to your child.

ATTUNEMENT

To be a mirror for your child requires you to spend time with him, taking pleasure and delight in him, accepting the range of his emotions, both negative and positive, and respecting and allowing his attempts to initiate and be separate. Being sensitive to a child's emotions and behaviours in a playful, accepting way is known as attunement. Muir, Lojkasek and Cohen describe this process as 'watch, wait and wonder' for toddlers and young children, and Gottman as 'emotion coaching' for older children. I have found their work incredibly useful in helping children, and will briefly outline both approaches.

The 'watch, wait and wonder' approach

'Watch, wait and wonder' builds the relationship between you and your child, helps them feel secure, and teaches them about emotions and relationships. It is also a reminder for us to slow down and simply appreciate the gift and glorious uncertainty of childhood.

Watch

Becoming attuned to your child requires that you watch her calmly and attentively. This may seem obvious, but can be surprisingly difficult when our minds are full of our own concerns, duties or anxieties. Also, a child's annoying behaviour can irritate us and make us focus on ourselves ('I'm feeling so angry') rather than on her ('I wonder why my child is so angry?'). It is a skill to be able to calm and contain ourselves so we can focus on our child.

Consider setting aside a regular time (perhaps fifteen to thirty minutes a day) to wholly focus on your child and to let them lead you. When your child is a baby or toddler, this would take the form of you getting down on the floor and simply responding to their lead. With older children, it is done in various ways from talking to playing.

Common to either approach is that we don't initiate, tell or show them what to do. Instead we let them lead the play or conversation, and we try to be reflective and supportive of their endeavours whatever they are. We don't tell them what to do or when they are doing something wrong, rather we listen and attempt to understand or imagine what it is like for them. Some parents find this supporting very easy and can tolerate their child doing their own thing even if it means watching them make mistakes. Other parents find it *incredibly* difficult to allow their child to initiate without stepping in and saving them from making errors.

If you are in the habit of taking the lead, the first time that you step back and simply watch and support them, your child may feel uncomfortable and start to do things to try to get you to take on the 'saving' role again. They may become anxious, or they may become angry, or they may try to provoke you to discipline them. Try to resist this urge (unless they are doing something unsafe).

Don't make suggestions or give hints, simply say, 'I'm just really interested in what you want to do/play/say', and keep gently but firmly repeating it in a calm way. Eventually they will take the risk of initiating in their relationship with you. And if they do initiate in unhelpful ways such as silliness or control, in your mind celebrate that they are at least initiating – annoying initiation is a much better teacher and self-esteem builder than calm subservience.

Wait

This is the next step in improving our attunement. When our child's behaviour concerns us, our first response is usually to react immediately to correct it. By waiting, even if only for a few seconds, it gives us time to consider our response first. A classic emotion management technique is to 'count to ten' before you respond.

Waiting also gives our child the chance to initiate a course of action rather than relying on a parent for guidance, which supports the development of self-esteem and separateness. For growth and learning, it is better that children are given the space to make mistakes (within reasonable boundaries), than to be given too little room to take a chance.

Wonder

What a privilege it is for us to watch our children grow. And isn't it amazing that the more we know, the more there is to know. We can't know exactly what is going on in their minds. There is no crystal ball, and there are no certain answers.

But we can wonder.

We can reflect on what is happening for them; we can use our own empathy to put ourselves in their shoes. Our attempts to understand our children help them to feel thought of (and more securely attached) – they know they are 'on our minds'. Our wonderings, if expressed gently, can also help our children understand themselves, and to learn that not everything can be perfectly understood or every problem solved. This is especially needed in the teenage years when many of their difficulties are quite complex, and at times the only way to resolve a problem is to grieve and accept the insolubility of it – this takes great emotional strength.

The emotion-coaching approach

As we have seen, one of our most important roles is to help our child become aware of their emotions and how to manage them. John Gottman's research suggests that parents who get involved in the emotional life of their children have more resilient children and teenagers. He coined the term 'emotion coaches' to describe parents who allow their children to express negative emotions and then help them learn to deal with these emotions. Underlying his approach is the idea that all *emotions* are okay and need to be expressed and tolerated, but not all *behaviours* are okay. Through research he identified parents who, though warm and positive people, were *unable* to effectively teach their children emotional intelligence. Broadly they fell into three groups:

- **Dismissing parents**, who trivialised or struggled to acknowledge their children's negative emotions;
- **Disapproving parents**, who punished or reprimanded their children when they displayed negative emotions; or
- **Laissez-faire parents**, who accepted and empathised with their children's negative emotions, but were unable to offer guidance or set limits on their behaviour.

Let's look at an example. Six-year-old Harry repeatedly wanders into the lounge room and says, 'I can't get to sleep.' He is clearly upset.

A *dismissing parent* might tell Harry that his reluctance is 'silly', that he has nothing to worry about, and may try to distract him with a funny story or by reading a book. In this case the emotion is not accepted as okay, but dismissed as if it didn't exist, and thus the parent is unable to coach Harry about how to deal with it.

A *disapproving parent* might tell Harry that they are sick of his behaviour, and may even threaten to punish him if he keeps it up. In this case the emotion is not only actively disapproved of as if it shouldn't exist, but the child is criticised and shamed for having it in the first place.

A *laissez-faire parent* might tell Harry that they understand his desire to stay up, but then would not know what to do. They might make a deal with him: 'Ten more minutes of TV, and then off to bed.' Here the emotion is acknowledged as acceptable and okay, but Harry does not learn how to understand and deal with it.

An *emotion-coaching parent* would begin by first accepting and then empathising with Harry's feelings ('Oh, sweetie. I can see you're upset about not being able to get to sleep') and then working with him to find a strategy to solve the problem.

Such emotion coaching is generally done in five steps:

1. First **reflect** on what the child is feeling and why. Is it anxiety about being alone? Fear of nightmares? Anger and frustration at missing out on being with his parents? A physical problem (eczema itchiness, fever etc.)?
2. On recognising the emotion, **accept** that like all emotions it is okay to feel that way, and see it as an opportunity for intimacy and learning.
3. **Listen** to the child's feelings, and let him know it is okay to feel that way perhaps by giving examples of times you have felt the same way (e.g. 'I used to get really angry when I wasn't allowed to stay up and watch my favourite show').
4. **Support** the child to find the words to label the emotion he is having, such as using the word 'worry' about being alone, or 'angry' about missing out.
5. **Explore** *with* the child strategies to solve the problem (don't tell him what to do), but at the same time **set limits** around what behaviours are okay and what behaviours are not okay. For example, you might say, 'It's hard to fall asleep sometimes. What could you do to help you slow down your mind and relax? (*Not* 'Go back to bed honey and count backwards from 100' or 'Breathe in and out slowly'.) Setting limits is important, too: 'Well, you can't stay up and watch TV – that's not an option. But how you try to fall asleep in bed is up to you.'

The emotion-coaching parent:

- Accepts the child's emotions (though does not give permission for unacceptable behaviour – acceptance of the emotion is not permission for the behaviour)
- Lets the child know they are understood, and in doing so helps the child understand themselves
- Provides limits and explores strategies to help the child discover that their emotions can be understood, and their problems can be solved.

CHAPTER 2

SEPARATION: MISSING OUT ENOUGH

As we saw in the previous chapter, children need enough attachment and affection from us to feel secure and so develop emotion regulation and confidence in relationships. Yet, ironically, although our core role is to be a secure base to which our children can always return, the ultimate purpose of providing this secure base is to help them leave us and find lives of their own.

In effect, parenting children well means they are able to take everything we give them and learn to 'parent themselves'. There is no greater investment you will ever make in money, time, affection and attention. And there is no investment over which you will have less control of the outcome. The ability to guide your child, in balance with the freedom to let her lead and become her own person (even if it is not what you would wish for her), is one of the most challenging of parental tasks. Your child is a glorious uncertainty to whom you contribute with the entirety of your being, yet with no guarantee of the outcome but a hope that though free to leave, she may return. Are children ungrateful at times? Too right! Will you get taken for granted? Absolutely! It is highly unlikely they will truly understand or appreciate what you have sacrificed until they have their own children.

In order to give our children the freedom to become themselves, we need to be as secure in ourselves as possible. At times they will use and abuse us as a tool to meet their needs. We, on the other hand, should *never* use our child as a tool to meet our own needs. We can *want* certain things from our child (love, affection, help, thanks), but if we start *needing* things from our child to make us feel better then it becomes so much harder for them to separate from us in a healthy way. The more secure we are, the easier it will be for our children to separate from us. As mentioned at the beginning of the book, if there is insecurity within a relationship, everyone feels unsafe and it is much harder to play, think, be curious and try new things.

Olivia

Olivia came to see me about her daughter, Megan. She had numerous concerns about her eight-year-old, but seemed most anxious about Megan's lack of verbal affection. 'She never says, "I love you, Mum," without me saying it first, and when she does say it, it's like a chore rather than something spontaneous.'

We explored why it was so important for her to hear this. As a child, Olivia's parents had never told her they loved her, and she remembered feeling unable to say it to them. The pain of this loss was still with her, and a few tissues later I asked her, 'I wonder if you want Megan to spontaneously love you, or if you need her to?'

Over the next few sessions she discovered the true extent of her own insecurity – that when she did not get Megan's spontaneous love she felt that something was wrong with her. We considered the pressure Olivia's anxiety put on her daughter, and how this would make it hard for Megan to even think about what she wanted. My work focused on helping Olivia understand this, and then developing her confidence in being 'good enough' to take the pressure off her daughter. As she needed her daughter's affection less, the affection gradually became more spontaneous and playful, and the insecurity within their relationship diminished.

THE NEED TO SEPARATE

The child's drive to separate from their parent and be independent of them (sometimes called individuation) can create difficulties because every move towards independence involves compromising the drive for attachment (the need to feel safe and secure). And it can create difficulties for the parent because every move towards letting go involves compromising their wish to protect.

The tension between our children's attachment and individuation drives creates much pain and confusion for them (and for us as parents). This is because fulfilling one wish means denying the other. Healthy resolution of the tug-of war between dependence and independence requires the child to give up the idea that they will get their needs met perfectly and completely, and instead accept that their needs will be met 'enough'. Thus they are not perfectly safe, but they are safe enough. And they are not completely independent, but they are independent enough. In essence they need to be able to say, 'I don't get everything I want, and I may even have to change what I want, but I get enough, and that is okay.'

When our children are infants, the balance between closeness and separateness is down towards the closeness end. But as they develop and experiment with the distance between themselves and us, the balance slowly shifts towards the separateness end. Think about how a child learns to crawl and walk, or how they are toilet trained – all major achievements of individuation. The walker first pulls herself up on furniture and pushes us away if we try to help as if to say, 'I can do it myself.' The toddler struggling to pull up his own trousers will say, 'I do it!' if we rush to assist. He is really saying, 'Go away. I don't need you to help me.'

This shifting of the balance occurs in fits and starts rather than in a smooth and continuous line. At times there will be a regression, where your child seeks out more dependency when he is sick or under stress. In times of stability, when he is feeling more confident, he is more likely to take bigger steps towards independence.

Moving towards independence and away from dependence always involves risk: the child is giving up the obvious and tangible benefits of dependence for the more obscure and uncertain benefits of independence.

Donald Winnicott had a lot to say about this process of individuation, and the importance of parents providing a 'secure base' for their children. It is from this secure base that children can take the exploratory and risky ventures into independence, knowing they have a safe and secure base they can return to if they get into strife. As an example, you can only climb Mount Everest if you are confident that your base camp staff can help you if you get into trouble, and will be there to support you when you return from your exertions. More secure bases allow for more secure separations.

The balance between being connected and being apart is a compromise that has to be worked on, negotiated and altered over and over again as children move towards becoming their own person. The child learns that his wishes cannot be absolutely fulfilled – he cannot get exactly what he desires every time he wants it. This is an important preparation for his adjustment to the wider world, where no one gets exactly what they want whether it be in relationships, health, looks, roles, possessions or hopes. At best, we can simply get enough.

It is thus inevitable that we will disappoint our children. What they want from us is everything, and this is something we simply cannot provide. It is crucial that we understand and accept this, otherwise we will be caught up in our children's disappointment. If you struggle emotionally when you disappoint your child, you may find that not only are you easily manipulated by him, but also that he may struggle to give up some of his absurd expectations of you.

The value of letting children 'work it out for themselves'

There are two important reasons why we must let them work out their own attachment–separation balance. The first is that if we butt in and tell them what they should do, rather than let them sort out a problem themselves, we deprive them of crucial learning experiences that will help them to develop competence, resilience and self-esteem.

The second reason we need to let them sort it out is to avoid unnecessary tension. If there is a conflict going on inside of them, it is wise to stay out of it. If we jump in and take one side of their argument, we will find ourselves caught in their battle. Consider, for example, the teenager who is in a rocky relationship and is trying to work out whether or not to stay with their partner. Now, if we intervene and take a side (e.g. 'You need to break up with them') one part of them will agree with us, but the part of them that wants to stay in their romantic relationship will fight us.

On top of this, their adolescent drive to individuate may mean they reject our advice simply because agreement would make them feel more dependent. Thus the unintended consequence of getting involved in their ambivalence may be to push our adolescent further towards their romantic relationship, and create conflict with us that could have been avoided.

The balance between holding on and letting go

In understanding our children's ambivalence about being connected and apart as they individuate, we also need to understand our own drives and how they influence our child's individuation.

In our early days as parents, we feel a surge of protectiveness towards the fragile and vulnerable human being in our care. Our first role is to 'not drop the baby' and to let no harm come to her (paralleling her wish to be safe and secure). However, as she grows, our role becomes one of allowing her to assert her autonomy and separateness.

Just like our child, we have two drives pulling us in opposite directions; to hold on and to let go. And just like our child, we have to accept a balance between these two extremes. We know we cannot keep our child perfectly safe, even though there is a part of us that desperately wants to. So we have to give up this beautiful but impossible fantasy of absolute protection, and accept that our child can only be 'safe enough'. Finding a balance between telling her what to do (saving her) and allowing her the freedom to take a chance and learn for herself (supporting her) is our job in a nutshell.

Over time, the balance shifts from holding on/saving to letting go/supporting. At the same time our child, through trial and error, develops his own sense of balance between the extremes of distance and closeness. This process is made more complex by the fact that the balance he chooses may be different to ours.

If our balance is more towards holding on and our child's is more towards being separate, he will feel that he is being dragged towards dependency, and will push away from us to gain more space. At the same time, we may feel that we are being forced to let go and take more risks than we are comfortable with, and we will fight to hold on tighter. The wider the gap between ours and our child's balance points, the greater the level of anxiety, dissatisfaction and conflict for all.

A further complication is the fact that each parent will have their own balance point between holding on and letting go, creating the potential for three points of conflict. Not only can a child be in conflict with each parent, but also the parents can be in conflict with each other.

Actively communicating and seeking a united approach between parents is essential to minimise conflict. Obtaining a united parental approach helps moderate each parent's position of balance; it is quite rare for one parent to be totally right and the other to be totally wrong. My experience when working with parents is that those who can work with each other despite differences in opinion usually have the best outcomes for their children. (See Chapter 8 for more on unity.)

Tips for balancing holding on and letting go

- Accept and celebrate your child's experimentation with different positions of dependence and independence. For example, when your child is a toddler, dinnertime is a time of mess as they play with the independence of 'doing it myself'. They may also play with dependence, acting as if they want you to handfeed them again. If you can accept this play and even celebrate their attempts, it helps them experience times of being both held and let go, and they will work out for themselves what they actually want.
- Set clear boundaries for experiences/behaviours that are

excessively dependent and independent. For example, if your toddler consistently plays with wanting to be handfed, in time you would put a boundary around this, letting them know that you will help them in some other way (e.g. cutting up the food), but that the days of 24/7 handfeeding are over. And if your teenager states they will only eat in their bedroom alone, you would let them know that you support them doing their own thing and are willing to discuss ways to help this happen, but that in your family you all eat together at the kitchen table.

- Forgive yourself, your partner or your child if any one of you goes too far in any one direction. We will all make mistakes at times, and repairing any problem and minimising shame helps to build confidence that things can be tried even if they don't always work out. We tend to learn faster and more deeply when things are repaired after a problem occurs.
- Talk about what works and what doesn't work. In general, if tension between two people can be talked about together, the tension will be lessened. If one parent thinks the other parent is creating too much risk by allowing their teenager to go to a certain party, talking about why this is and coming up with a united position indicates that a compromise has occurred with a sharing of the burden of the decision. If your fifteen-year-old comes home intoxicated, there will be less blame, and it will be easier to repair. If on the other hand one parent says, 'Have it your way', there will not only be unspoken resentment, but in the event of it going pear-shaped, the 'I told you so' will make everyone more defensive, make repair much less likely, and make trusting each other in the future more difficult.
- Be prepared to change – to find new positions of balance – as your child develops. You may have a clear idea about what you think is best for your child, but you are not your child. They will increasingly have their own ideas about what they want, and they won't necessarily be the same as yours. Your child is a wondrous uncertainty, and the terrifying truth is that in the end they will become their own person, just as you did.

GRIEF AT MISSING OUT

The experience of having two opposite drives at the same time is known as ambivalence, and comes with opposite emotions ('mixed feelings'). As adults we are often ambivalent and have mixed feelings. For example:

- We want to go to work, and we don't want to go to work.
- We want to be in a relationship, but we want to be out of the relationship.
- We have feelings of love for a person, but also feelings of frustration, anger, disgust and even hate for that same person.

Our children also experience ambivalence. Awareness of this confusing and mixed emotional state in our children can help to explain some of their seemingly absurd behaviours such as:

- Hugging their baby sister one minute, then hitting her the next.
- Crying to be picked up, but then wriggling to be put down when you do.
- Behaving like independent adults one moment, then acting like dependent infants the next.

Such behaviours can be quite frustrating for parents, and usually lead us to ask the question, 'Well, what *do* you want?'

The solution to ambivalence is not black and white; in fact you can't solve ambivalence, only accept it. As we saw earlier, our children have to gradually develop the ability to give up their desire for total fulfilment of their drives, and instead accept that they can only get 'enough'. The word 'enough' is possibly the most important word in our child's emotional and relational growth, and also in our own development as parents. Though our child often wants 'everything', healthy development eventually leads them to accepting 'enough'.

What do our children want?

Here are some of the wishes our children have, unconscious and conscious, and the compromises they need to accept:

- They wish to be perfectly safe through being perfectly connected to their mother, only to discover that there is a distance between them that is both physical and psychological, and that there will always be some distance and some danger.

- They wish to control their mother and make her do what they want, only to discover that their mother has her own mind and her own desires that they cannot control.
- They wish to be 'special': to possess and be the only one in their mother's life, only to discover that she has other 'objects' that she is connected to such as a partner, other children, friends, and tasks that must be completed.
- They wish that if they can't be the only one, then they must be the most important one in their mother's life, only to discover that they are only one of many important people in her life.
- They wish to have discomforts immediately resolved, only to find that they may have to wait, or that some discomforts cannot be resolved, only gotten over.
- They wish to be able and allowed to do whatever they want, only to discover that there are limits to their power and their freedom.
- They wish to be perfect at what they choose to do, only to discover they cannot be perfect.
- And then if they cannot be perfect, they wish to be the best, only to discover that this, too, is not always possible.
- And once they begin socialising beyond their family these wishes involve their friends and other adults: the wish to be 'special', the best, the only one, not having to share, and to be able to control their friends. And though they are wonderful, once again they find that they are not special, but are simply one of many.
- As they get into their teenage years their thinking becomes more abstract. They then have to deal with the issues of existence: they will one day die, every important relationship will end, they have to discover meaning and purpose for themselves, and they are fully responsible for their own actions. These existential truths cannot be solved and have to be accepted – a lifelong process.

Children experience having their wishes dashed throughout their development. In fact, as we saw earlier, one of our jobs as a parent is to gently and gradually disappoint our children, which helps them to grieve the loss of their unattainable wishes, and to develop newer and more helpful ones. Despite knowing this, as parents it is still painful to watch our children suffer in this way. We often wish to spare them from the pain that we have probably experienced ourselves as children and adults. However, the suffering of grief cannot be avoided – one of the truths of living. Understanding the process of grief can help explain some of our children's behaviour.

Stages of grief

When we lose something that is important to us, whether it be a person, a thing, or a wish, we all go through certain stages that together make up our experience of grief. These 'stages of grief' were initially developed by Elizabeth Kubler-Ross to explain how people respond to the loss of someone through death. However, these stages also work with other losses, and are applicable to children and adults. The stages are:

- Shock and disbelief
- Bargaining
- Anger
- Sadness
- Acceptance.

Shock and disbelief: 'This isn't happening'

Children's most immediate response to a loss is to be shocked that what they want is gone, or to deny or lack awareness that it has actually gone. This shock and disbelief alters the reality they find themselves in, and protects them from the painful awareness of the loss. As adults we understand how the world works and what is and isn't possible, and so we tend not to get stuck in denial for long. But children (especially younger ones) lack the cognitive skills and experience to assess 'reality', and can remain in denial for a long time. While this is a very effective way of coping with their loss in the short term (enabling them to retain the fantasy that their wishes are still met), in the long term it prevents them from learning more mature ways of coping.

Bargaining: 'How can I get it back?'

The next step is to try to do something to reverse the loss – to bargain our way out of unwanted situations. As an example, children often blame themselves when parents separate, and some try to 'repair' the parental relationship by being 'really good', controlling their parents by arranging meetings, trying to sabotage a new relationship, creating havoc or even being sick to get the parents together again.

As another example, if a child feels insecure because his friend has other playmates, he may attempt to monopolise his friend's attention with controlling behaviour. This can be done in various ways, including seemingly nice ways such as giving gifts or always doing whatever the friend wants to do, or in less nice ways such as making him feel guilty or punishing him when he chooses to spend time with others. In the short term this helps him feel like the 'special one' to his friend and avoids the pain of missing out or having to share his friend with others. However, this bargaining is not only exhausting and time-consuming but also unlikely to work in the long term. Most children who experience being controlled by another person will avoid that person, unless it is behaviour they are used to from their own parent.

If his bargaining is somewhat successful and he doesn't have to share the friend, this is also problematic for his development, since he doesn't learn to accept that he is not the 'only one', and is driven to keep on using control and bargaining to cope when things don't go his way.

Anger: 'It shouldn't be like this!'

If we want something but know that there is nothing we can do to get it, the next stage is to be angry.

Our children frequently experience missing out (a sibling gets something they wanted, a parent doesn't want to play when they want to, a friend ignores them, they don't get chosen for a team, they get told their effort wasn't good enough), and the rage they feel because of this can be overwhelming to them.

The tantrums of the 'terrible twos and threes' make sense when you consider their development and the grief they are going through. Toddlers are gradually becoming more aware of their wishes and desires, and that these are coming into direct conflict with the reality they find themselves in.

From a developmental perspective, expressions of anger are wonderful. They signal that our children are becoming aware of the gap between what they want and what they get. It is vital that they experience their anger, because by doing this they are learning about their emotions and the various ways of dealing with their anger. It also gives us the opportunity to put limits on our children's behaviour so they learn how to make sure that their anger is not destructive to the people they love.

While the emotion of anger is something to be welcomed, parents need to contain a child's more destructive behaviours. One parent told me a mantra he had developed to address his son's aggression: 'It's okay to feel angry, but it's not okay to be nasty.' This echoes Gottman's idea that while all emotions are okay, some behaviours are okay and some behaviours are not okay.

In those early years, children need to be allowed to express rage. And you need to understand and contain their rage without becoming defensive or becoming enraged yourself. If *you* can handle it, *they* can handle it. They will learn that their aggressive impulses can be managed, and that they are not 'all powerful' – they cannot destroy you, and there is nothing they can do to make you reject them. If children struggle to express their anger and get over it, then they may get stuck and keep using anger as a way of dealing with their disappointment (the latter half of this chapter deals with anger in more detail). Ways to help children soothe themselves when they are overwhelmed by strong emotions will be discussed further in Chapter 3.

Gary

When Gary's nine-year-old son, Mark, expressed anger, Gary had trouble controlling his own rage. One afternoon, Mark went into a meltdown when his younger brother came home with a packet of lollies after accompanying his dad to the shops. 'It's not fair! Where are mine?' He worked himself up and started saying hurtful things to his father, 'You never do nice things for me! I hate you!' and then hit his father's leg. In the past, Gary had generally reacted to this by yelling back at him with something like, 'Well I won't do nice things for you when you behave like that! Go to your room! I don't want to see you until dinner.' Mark would usually go to his room and start trashing it, at which point his father would barge in and begin yelling, and Mark would scream back – the rage escalating until Gary stormed out and left Mark sobbing.

This time, Gary tried to do something different. He took a deep breath, counted to three, and then said, 'It must feel awful that you missed out, and you seem quite angry at me. It's okay that you're angry, Mark, but it's not okay to hit me.' Mark was still angry, but his rage subsided quickly, and within a few minutes his father was able to distract his boys by taking them outside to play basketball.

Sadness: 'I don't want it to be this way'

If your child accepts that the loss has happened, accepts that they can't do anything to reverse it, and has experienced anger, the next stage for them is to enter into the deepest work of grief: the gradual and painful surrender of their wish.

When someone close to us dies or leaves us, those thousands of invisible threads of connection we have with them become stretched and create immense pain. Cutting those ties can be considered the work of grief. Though we don't want to, we have to let go and feel the sadness of the loss – a very gradual process. Months later we may be reminded of being with the one we have lost, and the sadness floods in as we remind ourselves that they are gone.

We can also lose an object, an idea or a wish, and though there may initially be denial, bargaining and anger, eventually we truly experience the sadness of the loss and this experience (when not tainted by residual denial, bargaining or anger) leads on to acceptance of the loss. In my experience where someone is stuck in sadness over a loss and can't come to acceptance, it's usually because anger, bargaining or denial has blocked them from fully experiencing the loss.

Acceptance: 'It's how it is, and that is okay'

Without acceptance, children are 'stuck' in denying the loss has taken place, trying to get what they want back, or in anger and disappointment that the loss occurred in the first place – which hinders further growth and development.

The same process occurs in adulthood. For example, when a partner leaves you against your wishes, the experience is intensely painful. At first you can't believe it, and then you may put energy into getting them back (phoning, texting, buying gifts). And when this doesn't work you feel angry and want to punish them in some way. And then there is the deep sadness as you cut the ties to the person. All these things can happen at the same time, or one by one. But until acceptance is reached, you are still connected to the ex-partner and are unlikely to be able to establish a healthy relationship with a new partner.

Why grief is important

Our children wish for many things they cannot have or that cannot be. But while they are stuck in the early stages of grief and don't accept their loss, it is hard for them to develop new and more helpful wishes that they *can* connect to that will aid in their development. We need to help them grieve and accept that some of their wishes cannot be, so they are freed up to grow and develop newer and more mature hopes, wishes, and dreams. And where they have two competing drives (ambivalence), they need to be able to grieve the loss of the wish for perfect fulfilment of those drives, and in doing so, come to accept that they get 'enough'.

The grieving process is also complicated by the fact that no one ever comes to 'perfect' acceptance of a loss, just 'enough' acceptance. The underlying wishes remain, but you accept that they cannot be. And because they remain, there is a tendency for them to come back and haunt us at times. The wish to be 'special' or the 'only one' is always present, and accepting that we can only get 'enough' of another person's affection and attention is a challenge that comes and goes throughout our lives. The wish to have one's mother to yourself or to be the most important child (sibling rivalry) has to be managed in an ongoing way throughout life.

Your child's age, temperament and whether she feels insecure or secure will influence how she negotiates the work of grief. Some seem to sail through their losses with little distress, where others intensely feel even the tiniest shifts in their relationships. Whatever your child's experience, it is crucial that you recognise that it is your *child's* job to grieve, suffer and accept – not yours. As we have seen, trying to protect children from suffering does them a grave disservice, denying them the opportunity for healthy growth. All you can do is understand what they are going through, support them, and *show* them how to 'get over' loss, by getting over your own ('modelling'). The first time your child misses out on a birthday invitation from a friend will cause them much grief (and probably some for you, too). You can't save them from this pain, but you can support them through it.

So, if you observe that your child is denying, bargaining, angry or sad, it may be that she is grieving a loss. This is where 'watch, wait and wonder' as discussed in Chapter 1 can be helpful (see page 29). Take the time to reflect on what it is that your child wants but can't have, and consider some way you can assist her be more aware of and accepting of the loss.

Sibling rivalry

One of the earliest losses a child experiences is not being the only one in his mother's life when a sibling is born. He may seem quite happy and helpful, and cuddle his little sister at first, but if you watch, wait and wonder, you will see the various stages of grief occur:

- At first he may behave as if the new sibling does not exist or will try to make them 'go away'. I have heard stories of little babies being covered in blankets, put outside and doors shut, and even being offered to family friends to take away with the words, 'We don't need her anymore.'

- Bargaining kicks in as he tries to draw his parents' attention back to himself (which may explain some of his 'helpfulness', too).
- He may begin to complain loudly and display anger when he sees his unique position slipping away. One mother I saw found that every time she breastfed her infant, her four-year-old would 'accidentally' spill something on the floor, and her two-year-old would jump on the baby's new toys.
- Sadness and distress may also increase, especially about little things that he would usually get over easily. He now seems to need extra hugs and attention to cope with the tiniest challenges.

Ultimately, most elder siblings get over the worst of their envy and grief by going through the above stages and eventually reaching a level of acceptance, but the mixed feelings about a sibling never entirely disappear.

DISAPPOINTMENT AND HATE AT MISSING OUT

When there is a gap between what we expect and what we get (the 'disappointment gap') we can feel a spectrum of emotions from irritation and frustration to anger and hate – the bigger the gap, the more intense the emotion. Since we cannot avoid disappointing our children, they will feel negatively towards us at times.

A child's disappointment gap can be large for two reasons:

1. She has reasonable expectations but we are not providing what she needs (our problem). For example, it is reasonable that children expect us to listen to them. If we constantly tell them 'Leave me alone' or 'I'm busy. Go away' then there will be a disappointment gap and our child will feel rage and an impulse to punish. If this is the case, we need to lift our game (see Part 2).
2. We are providing what is reasonable, but her expectations are unreasonable (her problem). For example, it is not reasonable for children to expect that we always agree to what they want. In this case, we need to be confident that our response is

> appropriate and to gently but firmly stand our ground. And our children either will continue to be disappointed in us, or they will 'get over' and accept that their expectation is the thing that needs to change. In this case their expectations may gradually be modified to something like, 'I expect my parent to listen to and consider my wishes, but they won't always do what I want.'

This process of getting over and accepting a change in expectations is similar to the process of grief in that it involves our child suffering, and that we can't do it for them – all we can do is understand and support them, and let them know we believe they can do it.

The importance of hate

When I use the word 'hate' in parenting sessions, some parents are quite relieved. One parent burst into tears when for the first time she was able to express her fear that she was a bad mother because sometimes she felt hate towards her difficult child. However, other parents are horrified and quite shocked. Another parent I was seeing visibly stiffened when I used the word in relation to her child's aggression, saying, 'Don't use that word! It's an awful word, no one should feel hate. He is just very frustrated.' But I disagreed with her and tried to explain why I thought the word hate was more useful for her in dealing with her son's emotions.

When animals are hurt (or threatened with being hurt), they tend to respond instinctively in one of two ways: they either run away from it or they retaliate against it (the 'fight/flight' response). As humans, we are often disappointed and hurt by others. The primitive and more instinctual part of our brain would have us immediately run away from the hurt, or attack the person who is hurting us. There is plenty of evidence that this part of our brain is activated when we are hurt, as shown in the following examples:

- When you are next disappointed and angry, notice what happens to your mouth and hands: you often grit your teeth and clench your fists.

- Our nightmares are often full of biting figures like wolves.
- Horror films are traditionally overflowing with 'biting' characters such as vampires, werewolves, snakes and spiders.
- The younger our children, the more likely they are to bite and hit when disappointed. The simple act of telling your toddler 'no' can very quickly result in quite intense rage and a physical response directed at you.
- If you do none of the above, you tend to physically distance yourself from the person who has hurt and disappointed you by walking away, looking away or turning your back on them.

It is unlikely we would have survived as a social species if we responded at an animal level and went around biting or hitting when others disappointed and hurt us. Fortunately we have evolved an alternative to biting and hitting: feeling hate. Hating allows us to convert the automatic impulse to physically retaliate into a psychological experience that can be experienced and dealt with in the mind. The toddler who was biting and hitting begins to use words instead. Most young children yell 'I hate you' to a parent at some stage. A primary school-aged child generally has better control over the intensity of their anger and of their behaviour, so is less likely to physically lash out at the person. But the impulse to punish is still strong and may be expressed in hurtful words, or the energy of the hate can be directed at objects (door-slamming, wall-thumping) instead of the person who has disappointed them.

Teenagers feel disappointment intensely (the emotion-regulation part of their brains is still developing, so they are a bit like turbo-charged cars without brakes!) and can be quite punishing of their parents, though this is often done in passive-aggressive ways such as eye-rolling, swearing under their breath, asking for help and then rejecting the help offered, and being resistant or oppositional. Their comments are often critical or sarcastic put-downs, 'What would you know?', 'Good one, Dad.'

When our children disappoint us (especially when they express their own hatred towards us), though we may have the feeling of hate and the impulse to physically punish them, we are adults so we have learned to restrain ourselves.

Emotions are not right or wrong, they simply tell us something.

- Sadness tells us that we have lost something important.
- Pain tells us that our body is hurting.
- Anxiety tells us we think we are in danger of losing something important.
- Hate tells us someone has disappointed us, that our expectations were not met.

So before we go further I want to be quite clear. When I use the word hate here, I am talking about the emotion or feeling of hate, and like all emotions it is neither right nor wrong, but simply telling us something. This feeling of hate is very important for us to understand, accept and get over. However, like rage, there must be a line between acceptable/unacceptable behaviour. It is quite okay for your children to feel hate towards you when you disappoint them. It is not okay for them to behave hatefully towards you such as screaming, swearing, teasing or hitting you.

Hate and relationships

The confidence to 'hate and get over it' is vital if our children are to develop close friendships and intimate relationships. The closer you get to someone, the more you expect from them. And the more you expect from them, the more they will disappoint you. And the more they disappoint you, the more you will feel hate towards them. To get and stay close to someone you need to be confident you can hate them and get over it by either:

a Changing what you expect if your own excessive expectations are the problem, and asking forgiveness from the other person if your excessive expectations have hurt them in some way, or

b Letting them know about your disappointment if them not measuring up is the problem and forgiving them if they apologise and it is appropriate.

If you can't do this, then closeness and intimacy will be difficult to achieve and maintain. This idea that we can feel disappointment and hate towards someone we love is quite challenging for some people to accept, but I would strongly assert that disappointment, hate and the impulse to punish are universal experiences within important relationships.

It is a common experience in families where the mother is the primary caregiver that the mother gets the most complaints and the emotional intensity (the most love and the most hate), and the father (of whom less is expected) gets fewer complaints and less emotional intensity. In healthy development, the child gradually experiences the disappointment due to their unmet expectations, truly feels hate, but is able to get over this and develop newer and more helpful expectations. Not all children develop the ability to hate and get over it, which creates problems for them as adults.

From adolescence onwards, women at times experience hatred from men who haven't been able to get over their absurd and excessive expectations of their own mothers (the term for this is misogyny). Such men haven't been able to modify their deeply and often unconsciously held beliefs about what women 'should' be like (i.e. able to anticipate and meet all their needs like the 'perfect mother') and find themselves repeatedly disappointed when their partners or other women in their lives don't measure up; high expectations leading to high disappointment. Confusingly, the more a woman tries to meet the needs of such a critical and complaining man, the more he identifies her as 'mother-like' and therefore as the one who *should* be meeting all his needs. The more he feels hatred towards her, the more he behaves in a hateful way (actively or passively). Trying to meet the unreasonable expectations of others doesn't reduce the disappointment gap; rather, it actually reinforces the unrealistic expectations and therefore increases the disappointment.

However, it is not just men who hate women; women can also feel hatred towards women. Disappointment within female relationships can be quite intense whether it be a same-sex relationship or an intense friendship. If unresolved in our earlier development, what women expect of the women in their life can be excessive and can also lead to high expectations and high disappointment.

Misandry, the hatred of men, is present though generally less intense than misogyny, possibly because children tend to expect less from their fathers (males in general) than their mothers. To complete the definitions, misanthropy is the hatred of everyone.

There is only one person a child is closer to and expects more of than their mother, and that is their 'self'. In my experience, the intensity of hatred a child shows towards a parent is only half the hatred they feel towards themselves. If a child cannot truly hate and get over their disappointment in their parents, they will find it even more difficult to get over the disappointment they feel about themselves. Long-term self-loathing (along with shame and self-criticism) is associated with conduct disorders, depression, self-harm, substance misuse, eating disorders, dissociative disorders and is a major factor in most personality disorders. Helping your child to confidently experience the disappointment and hate of missing out, and to get over it, is one of the most important ways you can help your child's development.

The three ways of dealing with hate

All of us at times can hate in different ways, but most children and adults have a particular 'style' or pattern of dealing with hate, and often that style is modelled and passed down through the generations.

Broadly speaking, there are three ways people deal with hate:

1. Denying hate
2. Hating without altering expectations
3. Hating and getting over it.

Denying hate

Those who hate but are unable to acknowledge their feelings are in deep trouble. They are of course churned up and affected by their disappointment, but keep the emotions out of their awareness. Children learn to cope in this way if they discover that the expression of hate creates insurmountable problems for the relationship with the one who has disappointed them. Children will deny hatred when they believe it will:

- 'Destroy' the person they love
- Lead to rejection from the person they love
- Result in punishment.

Hating will 'destroy' the person they love

This can happen when a parent becomes deeply distressed with their child's normal expression of hatred. One single mother I worked with had been horribly abused by her ex-partner. When her four-year-old son yelled at her over being told 'no', she often froze up and became unable to think – at times even cowering and weeping. Her son would then become highly distressed and frantically try to comfort his mother. The young boy discovered it was not safe to be angry at his mother because his rage was too powerful, and his mother was unable to stand up to him. It took a lot of work with a domestic violence counselling service for her to be strong enough to cope with aggression, and much parent–child therapy for them both to discover that his rage was not something to be feared.

Hating will lead to rejection from the person they love

This can happen if the parent rejects and withdraws from the child when she expresses her rage. A father I was working with had his own issues with anger after being raised by a punitive and cold parent. He feared his own rage, and would withdraw quickly if he felt any anger, avoiding it and thus not being able to resolve it. When his daughter expressed any disappointment or frustration in him, he would leave the room or the house, only returning when she rang him to apologise. Though this meant there was little active conflict in the home, unfortunately his daughter was left feeling rejected and blamed for upsetting her father, and quickly learned to be a 'good girl' who should never cause a problem or complain. This developed 'false self' kept her father happy but left the girl with unresolved and unresolvable feelings that she had to hold inside. Her disappointment couldn't be thought about or spoken about with her father, but simply pushed away. It was dangerous to hate as it led to her being rejected and losing the one she loved. Her father's inability to tolerate his child's rage meant his child had to hold it all inside.

Hating will result in punishment

This can happen if the parent punishes the child in a way that leads him to become too afraid to express hatred for fear of retaliation. I worked with a young boy who was extremely inhibited and always looking for direction from the adults in his life. I always wondered why the boy was not more playful and able to take risks. It took many sessions for the mother to be able to admit that she had a problem with her own rage. She would aggressively yell at her boy whenever he made mistakes, and was excessively defensive and aggressive if he ever complained or was disappointed. He had learned to suppress his own desires and expectations because it was simply too dangerous to show frustration, let alone hate.

All three approaches to suppress hate work in the short term to decrease children's experience of danger, but in the long term lead them to being unable to explore the gap between what they wanted and what they got – to express their disappointment and then get over it. As therapists know too well, disappointment and hatred do not magically go away – they are simply pushed aside for a time.

Repressing emotion takes a lot of energy, and it often surfaces when people get distracted, tired, sick, intoxicated or stressed. And when it pops up, it tends to be directed at whomever is closest at the time, rather than at the person who was perceived as disappointing them in the first place. Children who have had a difficult day at school, for example, often blow up at their parents when they get home. And in separated families, it is often the parent who is the main carer who receives most of the child's expressed disappointment (due to both higher expectations leading to higher disappointment, and being in the wrong place at the wrong time).

People in deep denial of their hatred run from closeness in

relationships and struggle to cope with any form of intimacy. When friendships or relationships get tricky and they begin to experience disappointment in the other person, rather than dealing with their disappointment (and facing their rage), they just move on.

In the worst case scenario, others don't value themselves enough to have expectations that can be disappointed. They believe that there is no point hating because they never get what they want anyway, and tend to go through life being taken for granted.

So if your children *can* hate you should feel some relief, as the inability to hate generally leads to significant problems in relating to others, with relationships tending to be superficial and short-lived, or marred by them being taken for granted or misused by others.

Hating without altering expectations

Most people have no trouble feeling hate when they are disappointed. They have expectations that they are more or less aware of, and these expectations when unmet lead to them feeling various levels of frustration, irritation, anger or rage.

Those who know they hate are very aware of their disappointment. Hating for them is a highly advantageous and even pleasurable way of coping with the gap between what they expected and what they got. They can blame the other person for getting less than they expected ('I don't have what I should have, and it's your fault'), but more importantly (and tragically) it means they don't have to alter their expectations. Their hate enables them to maintain the fantasy, 'I *should* be great! I *should* be special!' If they got over their hate, they would have to change what they expected, and accept ideas like 'I can only be good enough', and 'I'm one of many and that's okay.'

The problem with not being able to stop hating is that it takes up a huge amount of energy, which means there is less available for a child to develop in healthier ways. Hating also means that a child's expectations are not modified, leaving the child stuck at the more immature level of having excessive expectations.

In a nutshell, those who can't stop hating are saying, 'My life would be great except for you.' Giving up their hate would mean having to accept where their life is at and that they are not special, which in some ways is our life's journey. It is far easier in the short term to continue to blame the other person and to hold onto the fantasy of specialness, but to do this the hate must be maintained.

Sarah

Fifteen-year-old Sarah was smart, sporty and an exceptional cellist. She had won numerous awards, and in some ways was a model student. However, she had no friends with whom she felt connected and found her schoolwork tedious and boring, which meant that going to school had become a source of increasing distress. On exploring with her what was going on, she expressed a litany of complaints. Her peers were stupid, immature and no fun. 'I could get along with them, but all they want to do is stuff around, and they're so boring.' Her teachers were lazy, didn't care, and were needlessly repetitive. 'I could learn what they are teaching in half the time, but they go on and on, and I just sit there bored out of my brain.' Everyone disappointed her, no one reached her standards, and she had an excuse for all her problems, and the excuse was always someone else's fault.

Over time in therapy we explored and exhausted her critical thoughts about others. She seemed to derive pleasure from pinpointing their failings, and spoke of her thoughts and dreams about herself in glowing and fantastic ways. It was difficult not to point out the obvious flaws in her comments, but I trusted that she would find these out for herself if I simply supported her and reflected back to her what she was saying and experiencing.

Sure enough, Sarah eventually began to express some doubts about herself: people didn't like her, she wasn't as smart as she thought she was, she felt nervous in groups, she worried a lot, and she didn't like herself that much. She began (with me and her parents as supportive mirrors) to look at herself, and struggled with what she saw. She started to grieve and painfully suffer: she wasn't as great or special as she hoped, and her lack of friends had less to do with her maturity and more to do with her not being able to fit in easily.

> Gradually Sarah began to criticise less, and to have more fun with kids her own age (previously all her friends were much older). School became more enjoyable, and she could tolerate the slow pace of learning as the school gave her extra advanced work to do. In short, she found pleasure in belonging and connecting as 'one of many', and was slowly able to give up the absurd wish to be the 'special one'.

Hating and getting over it

Being able to truly hate and get over it requires people to become aware of the gap between what they wish for and what they get. And with this awareness comes the possibility, through grieving, to gradually accept and modify their expectations. This process occurs over their entire development, and is a skill to be learned and honed over time. Those who are more skilled at getting over disappointment find that their friendships are easier with not only their family and their friends, but with themselves. They also have a larger reservoir of energy available to them to explore, play and take risks, and they experience more joy as it hasn't been stolen by their disappointment. Modifying their expectations, they accept more and blame less.

If the gap between what they expect and what they get is too big, they can confidently feel hate and get over it if they realise their expectations are too high. Or if their expectations are reasonable and the other person isn't measuring up, they have the confidence to listen to their feelings of disappointment and assertively act appropriately. Wouldn't we want our adult children to confidently feel hate if mistreated or cheated on by their partner, and confidently act by leaving the relationship if it was appropriate? Wouldn't we want our ten-year-old son to be able to feel anger if someone breaks or takes his favourite thing, and assertively demand its repair? Wouldn't we want our fifteen-year-old daughter whose classmates were criticising her good friend to feel affronted and be able to say confidently, 'Hey, that's my friend you're talking about'? If we want our children to be able to manage their disappointment and anger, the best way for them to learn this is within their relationship with us, their parents.

GETTING OVER GRIEF AND HATE

When children (or indeed any of us) are confronted with the emotional pain of grief and hate, it is like an obstacle in the way of their development. They have two options: they can try to avoid the pain of loss and disappointment ('moving on') or they can find a way to get over it ('getting over').

Moving on

Moving on is the easiest option in the short term for our children and for us. The grief or hate is not addressed but bypassed or avoided. This can be done by using a distraction such as food, a gift, watching TV or playing a game, or by avoiding situations that might result in grief or loss. The pain is only briefly experienced and then left behind. The difficulties are effectively dismissed as if they never happened. An example of this is the tendency to try to prevent siblings from losing or missing out. Some parents turn themselves inside out to be 'fair' to avoid the grief and disappointment that is often expressed. And rather than sitting with their child's suffering, the parent finds substitutes in toys, food or activities to pacify their child's distress. Of course, if the parent is busy or under stress, using distraction can be an effective way of getting through a tough moment more easily. However, if moving on (avoiding, dismissing or distracting) becomes a regular pattern of coping with grief and disappointment, it stops their children from learning important lessons and in the end makes them weaker when it comes to managing their own emotions. It also makes them vulnerable to needing to use distractions as a way of coping with emotions for the *rest of their lives*! (Think TV, social networking, alcohol, smoking, drugs, gambling ... the list is endless.)

Claire

Seven-year-old Ben had marked difficulties when it came to managing his emotions. I saw him once when he was angry about missing out on an expected birthday invitation from school (always a painful experience)

> and was pulling apart his favourite toy in my rooms. My response was to reflect to him, 'It's so hard to be left out; that must feel really awful.' This resulted in the boy settling and beginning to cry gently (a positive if you remember that sadness is the work of grief), but it also resulted in his mother, Claire, looking quite distressed. She immediately pulled a toy from her bag and gave it to Ben, saying, 'Forget about the party, we're going to McDonald's that day anyway.' Ben suddenly perked up, his agitated activity returned and he started to dance around the room singing 'I'm going to McDonald's! I'm going to McDonald's!' Claire turned to me with a look of relief and whispered, 'Phew! Crisis averted!'
>
> It was many months before Claire could tolerate and supportively sit with her child's distress rather than try to immediately move on and save him from his emotions.

Getting over

In the short term this is the hardest option. It involves approaching the ragged peaks of emotional pain like a mountain-climber; getting right up close to them, feeling them and finding a way to climb over them. The bigger the pain, the more strength and effort it takes. However, once the obstacle is climbed, your child not only builds up their strength but also their knowledge of how to get over problems. They will never 'enjoy' grief and disappointment, but they won't be terrified of them, and will be able to say, 'I know how to get over this.'

As parents, you cannot save your child by doing the work of 'getting over' for them; only they can do this. You cannot grieve *for* them, and you cannot hate *for* them. You can support them and encourage them as they do it themselves, and celebrate with them when they climb their 'mountain'. And you can model the ability to get over difficulties by facing your own.

> **Liam**
>
> Liam was nine when he discovered that the man he called 'Daddy' was not actually his father – an older cousin had let it slip during an argument at Christmas lunch. Liam's mother and 'growing-up' dad had been planning

on telling him for years, but there never seemed to be a good time. 'We just didn't want to make him upset.' His biological father was overseas and was unaware that Liam was his child.

Liam at nine came face-to-face with a mountain of grief: 'Who is my father?', 'Am I part of this family?', 'Does my dad really love me as much as my half-brother?', 'Why did they lie to me?', 'Who can I trust?' He had mixed feelings and was variously shocked, anxious, angry and sad.

His mother and father also had mixed feelings: guilt, discomfort to see their son suffering, defensiveness when they felt attacked leading to further guilt, anxiety about how the news would affect their relationship, as well as love and hope. Their approach to Liam's grief and all its attendant emotions was to dismiss and minimise them. 'He'll be okay. No need to go on about it. Just give it a few months.' However, when I became involved there had been many months of tension and distress with little improvement. All had tried to move on, but the emotions kept popping up.

Initially I met with the parents alone to help them develop a united understanding of Liam's difficulties and how they could help him. Then we brought Liam into the sessions, and when the issue of his father came up we simply listened to his thoughts and emotions, and I supported (and intervened a few times) to help the parents sit with their son's feelings rather than jump to defend themselves against their son's accusations.

When the rage of Liam's disappointment had been exhausted, we were then able to discuss the story of how Liam was born, why he hadn't been told, and the parents were able to apologise. His questions about his birth father were answered as much as they could, and when Liam asked if he could talk to his biological father the parents said they would help if that is what he wanted. Liam said he didn't want to right now, but might want to later.

Over the next few months his parents supported Liam's grief: helping him face and 'be with' his sadness and anger, listening to his questions and comments, not becoming defensive, answering where they could, and doing all the practical things that let him know he was loved and valued. Over time, the scores of little shared experiences that enabled Liam to face and 'climb over' his difficult thoughts and feelings helped him to get over his grief and he was stronger for it.

CHAPTER 3

THE AMAZING BRAIN

We have seen how the drives for attachment and separation influence our child's emotional and social development, but I want to go a bit deeper now and explain the role of the brain, as this understanding has some crucial implications for how we are best able to help our children's development.

THREE BRAINS IN ONE

As we saw in Chapter 1, the brain can be thought of as having three 'layers' or sections: the reptilian brain (the brain stem); the mammalian brain (the limbic system) and the human brain (the cortex, particularly the frontal lobes).

The reptilian brain is the smallest and innermost layer. It's all about survival, and controls functions such as heart rate, breathing, eating, reproduction, arousal level, sleep, and the fight/flight response. It is also the most ancient layer and is the part of the brain that we share with reptiles, hence the name.

The mammalian brain is a relatively small ring of tissue that circles the brain stem. It plays a major role in our drive to nurture and form relationships. It is a more recent evolutionary addition and is shared by all mammals, which have in common the intense nurturing and protection of their young, hence the name 'mammalian brain'. It, too, is ancient and is strongly interconnected to the reptilian brain.

The cortex is the highly developed and massive outermost layer of the brain. It contains billions of neurons with trillions of connections and is the most complex structure in the known universe. It has a number of different areas, but uniquely in humans (hence the name 'human brain') includes the massive frontal lobes. These cortical areas are involved in the higher brain functions such as thinking, language, judgement, planning, logic, consciousness, creativity and impulse control. It has sometimes been called the modern brain.

The human brain

In general, the human brain is the thinking part of our brain, and is smart, flexible and aware. It enables us to:

- **Solve problems** and plan for the future rather than merely react to what is happening in the present.
- **Be self-aware** and reflect on ourselves. Another term for this is mindfulness – the ability to observe our own thoughts and feelings as if we were looking at ourselves in the third person.
- **Have self-control** i.e. restrain feelings and drives that are considered unacceptable or inappropriate.
- **Use logic and reason** to make sense of the perceived world – find meaning and attribute causation to experiences.
- **Use language** to understand and manipulate ideas in symbolic ways.

The mammalian brain

The mammalian brain is less flexible and 'smart' than the human brain, but has more influence on emotions and behaviours. It is responsible for:

- **Developing patterns in relationships and feelings.** Once these patterns are developed, the mammalian brain tends to ignore any new experiences that don't fit the expected patterns. This is why it can be so hard to learn new ways of feeling and relating, and why most of us predictably repeat the same relationship successes and mistakes.

- **Helping to soothe the more primitive reptilian brain.** In Chapter 1 we saw that our first drive was to be safe, and that our way of feeling safe was to be securely connected to an attachment object. At a brain level, when we perceive that our survival is threatened, our reptilian brain is activated and its solution is generally to fight or flee the threat. The mammalian brain offers an alternative to fighting or fleeing: to seek out its attachment object to be soothed and protected by it. Your child's attachment behaviours (such as controlling, provoking, being helpless and creating conflict) are unconscious patterns created by the mammalian brain.

The mammalian–human brain connection

The mammalian brain operates at a nonverbal and relatively unconscious level, yet is a powerful motivator of behaviour. When it is activated, its diffuse connections (if unrestrained) can overwhelm the human brain, making logical thought and planning much more difficult. In times of insecurity, the ancient mammalian brain can completely switch off our thinking, leaving us as one big ball of emotional reactivity. Understanding the way these two different parts of the brain work can help us to understand our children's behaviour in times of stress. It is not logic that drives how we respond to a stressful situation but the feelings we have.

Charlotte

Charlotte, nine, is smart, attractive, good at sport, has a nurturing, well-off family, and a number of friends who like her. On all objective counts she has a lot going for her and very little to complain about. However, Charlotte constantly complains that she has missed out. When her sister is given some new clothes, Charlotte feels it is unfair and starts to sulk. Her parents tried drawing up a list of each child's clothing to show that they had an identical amount. But of course despite this chart, Charlotte still complained the next time her sister received something.

Her parents had been trying to use logic to help her see that her responses were unreasonable, but this was having little impact on Charlotte's behaviour and emotions. Her difficulties were not due to her human brain not working properly (when calm Charlotte could logically identify that her sister didn't get more than her), but because her emotional insecurities (mammalian brain) were so powerful that even small differences led her to feel she was missing out.

Understanding that her response was strongly driven by the long-term insecurities and disappointment patterns of her mammalian brain helped her parents see that logic wasn't going to help. Instead, they learned to mirror (reflect) Charlotte's emotions ('I can see you are feeling upset about this') and to support her (see Chapter 10) instead of reacting to them. They also learned to expect change to be slow, which helped them to be less disappointed when her old patterns popped up at times.

The mammalian brain develops rapidly over the first couple of years of life, processing experiences and emotions and creating patterns about how to feel and respond in different situations. The involuntary nature of these patterns makes sense when we are feeling insecure and require a rapid response (e.g. 'I don't feel safe' = cry for mummy). The power and immediacy of the reaction is less helpful in a situation that requires thoughtfulness and a tailored and modified response, and where reacting may make things worse.

In contrast, the human brain develops very slowly, and continues to do so into the mid-twenties for women, and late twenties for men. Progressive improvements in thought, logic and judgement (maturity) allow children to reflect on what is happening and how they are feeling about it, and to choose the best option for a given situation. This development partly depends on genetics and temperament (we can't do much about this), and partly on how often they experience opportunities to keep their mind switched on (this is the stuff we can influence). Being chronically insecure, worried, angry or sad makes it hard to learn new things.

Jasmine

Four-year-old Jasmine was walking to kindergarten with her mother. While waiting to cross the road she suddenly heard the screech of tyres scaring her (reptile brain), to which she responded by jumping behind her mother's legs (mammal brain). Her mother picked her up and soothed her and they continued on their way. A rapid reptilian/mammalian response was very helpful in this case.

Once at kindergarten, Jasmine began to feel unsafe when her mother was about to leave (reptile brain), and although she went to her mother to be soothed (mammal brain) she still didn't want her mother to leave. A reptilian/mammalian brain response alone was not helpful in this case.

Her mother hugged her, used her own human brain to think about the problem, and then gave Jasmine an idea: 'I'll be here waiting when kinder is finished. I know you can do it.' Jasmine was soothed enough by her mother's hug to be able to hear this idea, was able to remember the last few times she went to kinder and her mother was waiting when she came out, and this thought combined with her past predictable experiences of reuniting with her mother after class enabled her to separate from her mother.

As children develop, their human brain not only becomes much larger and wiser due to both brain growth and the effect of experience and problem-solving, but it also develops stronger neurological connections with the mammalian brain. The gradual connection and restraining of the mammalian brain by the human brain is a key part of the development of emotional self-control, and the skill of 'reflecting' or 'mindfulness', which is the ability to think about what you are thinking, feeling and experiencing. The weaker the connection between the human and mammalian brain, the less the mammalian brain is restrained and the more a person reacts at a mammalian level rather than *reflects* at a human level.

Finally, when your child is having a meltdown, remember that controlling emotions is one of our greatest challenges as human beings, and that there is a neurological basis for the meltdown. Our ancient brain (with its reptilian and mammalian layers) is situated at the very centre of our brain, and is the first to receive all our sensory perceptions (vision, hearing, touch, taste, smell). As an example, when we hear a loud bang or hear 'no' (both being a potential cause of distress), the auditory nerve rapidly sends this message to our brain, and its first stop is our reptilian/mammalian layer. Almost immediately these ancient parts start up automatic responses based on past patterns and on limited information. These responses occur so quickly that we are already responding before the signal from our ears even reaches our cortex (human brain). Then our cortex has to make sense of the signal (taking further time) and then decide on an appropriate action (more time again), by which time we have already been responding in a reptilian or mammalian way for a second or two. Before we are even thoughtfully aware of what the problem is, we are already responding.

This means our human brain is always playing catch-up, trying to rein in and restrain our more primitive responses after they have already been set off. At times our reptilian and mammalian responses are so strong that it's hard for the human to get a leash on them and pull them back. This is not an excuse for bad behaviour, but it is certainly an explanation for why it can be so hard at times for our children to choose wisely – their primitive brains have already made a choice and run with it for a second or two before their human brain is even aware.

The reptilian brain

The reptilian brain is the oldest, deepest and, when activated, most influential part of our brain. Its key role is survival, and it is responsible for our appetites for food and sex, and for the fight/flight response. When our reptilian brain is fully activated and unrestrained, our minds turn off and we go into autopilot. Fear in particular is a 'mind killer'. When your child is terrified, their thoughts cease to have any effect on their behaviour – fear takes over. Anger also kills the mind. When a child is in a rage she can say and do things that are outrageous and destructive even to her own interests because she simply isn't thinking. As for sex, the French call orgasm *la petite mort* (the little death) – a metaphor for the loss of all sense of time and even of one's self. And people who binge or overeat often describe the experience as losing themselves and any sense of time.

Because the reptilian brain is so primitive, it frequently confuses emotions and drives. For example, if a toddler suddenly chases a ball towards a busy road, his terrified mother may grab him and start yelling angrily, 'Don't you ever do that again!' The parent's response is an angry one, but the driver underneath it was fear for their child's safety. As another example, people who binge or comfort-eat will often find this behaviour is triggered by anxiety or anger that they are trying to smother or 'stuff down'.

The reptilian brain is generally quiet and relatively inactive when your child feels safe and secure, but when it is activated it takes over brain functioning and focuses all the senses, attention and behaviour on the perceived survival need. Sex and violence are deeply central to our primitive drives (just go to any cinema and see what is playing), to which can be added the equally powerful need for survival and food. And all of these have the ability to take us over and turn our minds off, for good or ill.

The ability to soothe your child and ultimately to teach your child how to soothe themselves in the face of these powerful drives is a core parenting role.

THE BRAIN HIERARCHY AND HANDLING STRONG EMOTION

Consider what happens in a teenager's brain if they are happily walking through the bush and they suddenly see a venomous snake on the path ahead.

First their reptilian brain overwhelms all other parts of the brain. All actions are aimed at survival as they immediately and mindlessly move away from the snake. They may jump backwards and hit the person behind them, possibly even hurting them, but their reptilian brain has no consideration for anyone or anything else as it is focused on survival. There is no mammalian brain function of nurturing or protecting others, and no human brain function of thinking about the situation.

Once the imminent threat of danger is over (they have moved away) and the reptilian brain is soothed, the mammalian brain kicks in. The teenager looks around for their friends, tells everyone to watch out and perhaps asks if everyone is okay – even giving or receiving reassuring pats.

Only when the mammalian brain feels secure does the human brain begin working. The teenager thinks about what happened, perhaps cracks a joke about it, starts to create a story and looks forward to sharing it with others, and may even take a scientific interest in the snake and look to see where it went. However, these human brain functions of story, humour and logic are only possible once the reptilian brain is soothed, and the mammalian brain is secured.

A similar hierarchy of brain function is apparent when a four-year-old has a temper tantrum on the supermarket floor after being told he can't have a lollipop.

The disappointed child is feeling enraged for not getting what he wants, and his reptilian brain takes over. There may be a combination of anger, hitting, biting, yelling and whining. Trying to talk to him when he's in this state is a waste of breath, and trying to touch him may result in you getting bitten. Like a reptile, he has lost his capacity to consider his mammalian connection to you, and he may even hurt those he loves in words or deeds.

Once the intense rage is over, his mammalian brain switches on and he will want to reconnect and be cared for. At this point, if we try to talk to him about what happened it may interfere with his mammalian brain becoming more secure. It is only when his reptilian brain is calmed and his mammalian brain is secured and cared for that his human brain turns back on and we can start to talk to him. We can ask him what happened, reflect with him ('It's hard to miss out on something you want') and generally help him to make sense of his meltdown. And once he is thinking, this is also the time to talk about a consequence for his behaviour. If he were just angry and distressed, no consequence would be necessary as it is always okay to be angry. But if he happened to hit you (and you had a 'no hitting' rule in your family with a consequence of no TV for twenty-four hours), then that would be the time to ask him what the cost is for hitting you, and if he doesn't know to let him know that he won't be watching TV until tomorrow. Of course this may result in another meltdown, but that's okay. You would just have to start again from scratch, celebrating his expression of anger and the fact that you are able to provide him an experience of missing out and being able to get over it.

Underlying all of the above is the need for you as the adult to *keep your human brain turned on*. If your child's tantrum results in your reptilian brain taking over, then the two of you will be like two reptiles having a go at each other – both saying and doing things driven by rage and inadequately modified by thinking and caring. So if you become reptilian in the face of your child's tantrum (and who doesn't at times?), you need to as quickly as possible soothe your own reptile, turn your mammalian/caring brain back on, and start thinking. Watch, wait and wonder is a catch phrase that helps some parents, because if you are wondering or reflecting, you are probably thinking with your human brain and so almost certainly not reacting with your reptilian brain.

Thus, in the face of your child's meltdown there is a hierarchy to follow:

1. Stay human and keep **your** thinking brain turned on.
2. Help to **calm** their reptilian brain.
3. **Care and connect** with (secure) their mammalian brain.
4. **Make sense** of (story) the experience and correct any unwanted behaviours for their human brain.

If children are calm and connected, soothed and secure, then helping them 'story' or make sense with their human brain is as simple as being curious and wondering with them what happened. Humans are generally pretty good at talking.

Caring for and connecting with children to help secure their mammalian brain is quite straightforward, involving various positive attachment behaviours as outlined in Chapter 1 such as touch, talking, helping, humour, playfulness, and sharing the experience.

But how do you soothe an angry or frightened reptile?

Soothing the reptilian brain

The brain stem is the first layer of the brain to develop, and is fully developed during the time in the womb. To the brain stem, the experience in the womb is the embodiment of safety and security. Anything that mimics the womb has the potential to be experienced by the brain stem as very soothing. Those things can become part of our approach when our child is out of control, and our child can learn to do those things for himself as part of his development of self-control. The advantage of these sensory approaches to soothing is that they don't involve many (or any) words – you can save those words and ideas for when our child is settled and his mind has turned back on.

Music

When in the womb, your child was constantly surrounded by 'music': their mother's heartbeat, pumping at a steady 60–80 beats per minute ('Shhh, shhh, shhh, shhh'), and the melody of her voice.

Music (especially with a heartbeat rhythm of 60–80 beats per minute) is often experienced as soothing. Relaxation music can help an anxious child fall asleep, and most teenagers use music for pleasure and to calm themselves when they feel distressed. Many parents instinctively 'shhh' their infants when trying to settle them, unconsciously mimicking a highly soothing experience. Singing nursery rhymes to a child is almost a universal practice with humans, and most nursery rhymes have a rhythm of 60 beats per minute. Music reaches the very depths of our being, and can help children and adults feel soothed and secure.

Movement

Along with the rhythm of music, the womb also has the rhythm of movement. Walking usually quietens a baby in utero, and the natural cadence of walking is 60 beats per minute.

Rhythmic movement is also experienced as soothing. We use rocking and walking (in arms or in prams) to settle infants, and later activities such as swinging, walking, jogging, dancing, martial arts and other rhythmic activities train a child to use physical ways to manage internal feelings. 'Take a walk to cool off' often works with angry teenagers, and parents can do the same.

Touch

The baby held in the womb feels a constant, firm touch that is not painful or discomforting. Firm but gentle touch is experienced as very soothing. Wrapped newborns fall asleep more easily than those without wrappings, and babies held in slings are often very content. Baby massage can also be a soothing and bonding experience for both baby and mother.

Toddlers' strong emotions are often literally out of control, and their rage can be quite frightening for them. Gently but firmly holding them is a good way to help them become calm. It is important, however, that you aren't angry or stressed when you hold them, as this will escalate their anxiety. (See note below.)

Once children are school-aged, our ability to hold them obviously decreases as their strength increases. However, firm touch is still soothing. Little children often seek out small spaces such as cubbies, tents, corners and under furniture when distressed. Being wrapped up in or under a heavy blanket can be deeply soothing, as can wearing a thick and heavy coat, and at times many teenagers 'doona dive' into their beds to settle themselves. 'Stress balls' are also useful: they are portable and when squeezed rhythmically use up some energy. Finally, if the child doesn't reject it outright, massaging their neck, hands or back is also very soothing, though feet can be too 'ticklish' for young children and too 'weird' for teenagers.

Note: If you are considering using holding I would add a note of caution. If your child has experienced being held in a terrifying and abusive way, or if when you are holding them you are furious and not in full control of yourself (i.e. you are in reptile mode), then such holding may trigger intense brain-stem survival fears and rather than being soothing, may escalate their brain-stem response. In either case, it is important to seek professional assistance to help your child get over their past experiences or to help you learn how to manage your own anger.

Physical comfort

In the womb, there is no hunger, thirst, sleep deprivation, or discomfort caused by temperature extremes. When an infant is distressed, we usually ask ourselves: is my baby wet or soiled, hungry, too hot or cold, in pain or overtired? We may not know the cause of the distress, but generally we look to see if there is a physical or environmental cause that we can remedy.

When our older children suffer discomfort we can't always impose a solution on them as we did when they were infants, but being aware of the possible reasons for their discomfort helps us be more understanding when they are sleep deprived, in pain, hungry, just had a falling out with friends, are overheated from running around, had too much sugar, are intoxicated etc.

Some things that can work to settle an agitated reptilian brain include:

- A drink of water (the colder the better, sucking on an ice cube helped a boy I was seeing)
- A small snack (lollipops or chewing gum seem to work well for many)
- A face washer or wipe to cool and clean the face, neck and hands
- A shower, bath or spa bath

- A twenty-minute powernap
- A quiet rest in a beanbag.

Ask your child to come up with other things that can be done at the beginning or end of a meltdown. Remember, these things need to be in place prior to the meltdown, as you want to minimise any talking while emotions are high (apart from brief supportive comments such as, 'It's okay', 'You'll be okay', 'You can do it', 'I'm here if you need me', or 'We'll talk when we're all calmer').

Safety

The experience in the womb is one of perfect safety and protection from survival threats. When an infant is distressed by a loud noise or a fright, the parent removes them from anything that is actually dangerous, and reassures them that everything is okay. Babies are very sensitive to how a parent is feeling and when a parent is frightened, the baby picks up on this and becomes frightened themselves. If their protector is scared, there *must* be something out there that is threatening their survival.

As children get older they remain sensitive to their parent's emotions, particularly anger or fear. It is crucial that in helping a child or young person to self-soothe, you are not scared or furious yourself. If your own fear or anger means *your* mind shuts down, then you will be unable to help your child's thinking brain control their emotional brain.

Of course, remaining calm and thoughtful is easier said than done. If you find yourself in the position of feeling helpless and thinking, 'What do I do now?' then you may be feeling insecure about your child's safety and she will pick up on this. Rather than soothing her, your uncertainty may escalate her fight/flight response. The greater your concern about her safety, the greater your emotion will be and in turn the greater her insecurity. Thus it is vital that when it comes to significant safety or aggression issues, you and the other adults responsible for your child have a clear plan. This 'safety plan' will be discussed in more detail in Chapter 5.

The 'bolt-hole'

A safe place of their own to escape to when upset, where no one else will intrude, is quite valuable in settings where mindless emotions frequently run high and a calming space is needed prior to addressing the problem. Adolescent psychiatry units in Melbourne have all developed these bolt-holes or safe spaces into which an agitated teenager can go to soothe themselves, and they work remarkably well at decreasing conflict. The staff in these units have discovered that talking works best only *after* the young person has been soothed. Many schools have also introduced a place where students who are beginning to lose control can go to settle themselves.

If needed, you and your child can also develop a safe space in your home with a large beanbag (which can feel a lot like being held), thick blankets, or comfortable pillows – small children may like a little tent they can get in. (You could use their bed as a bolt-hole, many children do, but this may have a negative impact on their sleep pattern as generally you would want their bed to be a place of rest and sleep rather than high emotion. Linking bed with emotions of worry, sadness or anger is not such a good idea.)

What you provide will depend on what your child needs and your own particular resources. It could be as small as a beanbag with a stress ball and a water bottle in the corner of a room, to a fully decked out spare room with an exercise bike or treadmill. The important point is that children know there is a safe place to go and that when they go there, they are expected to try to settle themselves down, and that they can later emerge with their minds 'turned on' and ready to talk.

The parent should also discuss with the child and agree on how and when the space is used (including the plan for checking in on them), which helps the parent stay confident, calm and thoughtful even when emotions run high.

As highlighted in the hierarchical approach to distress (page 73), once *you* are calm and your young person begins to feel calm, then you can both move on to 'securing', and once they are cared for you can wonder with them, human to human, about what happened.

Securing the mammalian brain

When our children are toddlers, their mammalian brains are weakly connected to their relatively inexperienced human brains, and we see the results of this in the tantrums of two- and three-year-olds. Children of this age are basically big balls of emotional reaction with little capacity to identify their feelings, let alone reflect on the cause and effect of those feelings. With maturity and development, our children increase their ability to think, and with this their ability to reflect on and restrain their feelings.

If a child is struggling with their emotion regulation, the problem may be due to their emotions or insecurities being too overwhelming, or their capacity for reflection (due to their age or delayed development) being too small.

Helping children manage overwhelming emotions

Some children are more insecure, emotional and easily triggered than others. This may be due to temperament and genetic make-up, or it might be due to past difficult experiences that have reinforced patterns of insecurity and emotional sensitivity, or it might also be a combination of both.

For these children, security can only be achieved by them having hundreds if not thousands of experiences where attachment needs are met enough in balance with separation needs, and their grief and disappointment at missing out are dealt with in a playful, accepting, curious and empathetic way. The most powerful relationship that can offer these repeated, consistent and predictable experiences is the one children have with their parents. It is why my first treatment intervention is usually to meet with the child's parents to obtain a united understanding and approach to their child's developmental needs. Donald Winnicott made the comment, 'Never do with a child that which you can teach a parent to do.'

Another approach to provide new experiences would be in a long-term psychotherapeutic relationship, but this would only be useful if the adults in the child's life were doing their part in helping to support the change being created in the therapist's room.

Using medication can also decrease the intensity of a child's negative emotions (especially sadness or anxiety), making them easier to restrain and work with. A minority of children for a number of reasons have excessive difficulties with their emotions, insecurities or arousal level. Medication doesn't do any 'developing' of the human–mammal brain connection, so should rarely be used without some other form of developmental intervention, and should never be used as a substitute for work to deal with the things causing stress to a child. You would never give medication for anxiety to a child who was being bullied before doing everything possible to stop the bullying. You would never give medication for depression to a child who was living in a home with high levels of verbal abuse – you would work on stopping the abuse.

Having said that, medication may help the child be less aroused or intensely emotion-driven, allowing the self-control they do have to be more effective, which in turn may have a snowball effect on increasing their self-control. Prescribing medication for children and adolescents should *never* be entered into lightly and without a comprehensive mental health assessment, with all options and risks/benefits carefully considered.

Helping children develop self-control

As we have seen, the skill of emotion regulation (sometimes called emotional intelligence) is pretty much a lifelong process. The last three chapters of the book deal with how parents can help children increase their human brain's ability to restrain their mammalian brain. They do this by offering predictable care (Chapter 8); setting boundaries which a child will gradually take on for themselves (Chapter 9); and by parents reacting less and reflecting more (modelling that emotions can be understood and managed, see Chapter 10).

When you feel frustrated at the slow rate of change in their emotional control, don't blame yourself. Firstly, it is your child's job to do the actual changing. We can support them and provide the things they need to develop self-control, but we can't do it for them. Secondly, you are up against a brain structure that has been around for a couple of hundred millions years which, on developing a pattern, resists alterations. It doesn't work at a language level, so words have a limited effect. If it is going to change (and it *can* change), it will be through hundreds, if not thousands, of repeated, predictable and consistent positive experiences.

PART 2

WHAT YOU NEED TO DO

CHAPTER 4

YOUR APPROACH IS EVERYTHING

As we saw in Part 1, having our attachment needs met is crucial to our emotional development, and these largely unconscious needs arise in the more 'primitive' parts of our brains. This means that the most effective way for your child to develop more healthy attachment patterns is not by talking about them, or even by seeing a psychotherapist (though this can be helpful in certain situations). Rather, your child's emotional development is best assisted through repeated and predictable experiences with the people who are most important to them – i.e. *you*. As their main caregiver you are in the best position to assist them, as you are their first and most potent teacher. They learn from you whether the relationship is running well or is under strain and there is conflict. In fact, the *most* learning occurs when a conflict or disagreement is experienced and repaired.

Now here's the rub: as parents, our teaching role begins with us being able to manage our *own* relationships and emotions. We can't expect our children to do something we can't do ourselves. There's no point telling our children not to smoke if we smoke, or to control their anger if we regularly throw wobblies, or even to do their chores if we are couch potatoes. We need to model the behaviour we want to see in our children.

If we have what might be described as a 'difficult' relationship with our child (something I constantly hear from the parents of teenagers), it is *our* responsibility to do something about it. As the mature adult, we need to set the standard that we want our children to follow. If we have unresolved grief or disappointment from our own experiences, we have to face that and get over it.

But in all of this, we need to keep in mind that though we often wish to save our children from harm and discomfort, what helps them most (especially as they get older) is if we allow them to work things out for themselves – if we trust them to cope. It can be very hard to watch our children make mistakes, but allowing them to do so is crucial for their development. Indeed, as we saw in Chapter 1, one of the hallmarks of effective parenting is maintaining a healthy balance between holding on and letting go. We need to give our children the freedom to become the people they will become while still supporting them and intervening when necessary. This means we need to be able to allow them to suffer setbacks, all the while being there for them, so they know we are on their side no matter what. They will hate us and love us, need us and reject us, help us and need help from us. And in all of these experiences they will find they are still loved and respected, that they are good enough, and that they will be okay.

But how do we achieve this balance between saving and supporting our children? A large part of it is confidence, which comes from understanding what children need for healthy development, and this is what I want to turn to in Part 2.

In my experience, children need to:

1. Feel safe
2. Have basic needs met
3. Experience unity
4. Have affectionate care
5. Have boundaries
6. Have carers who reflect more and react less.

As you read about how to meet these needs in the following chapters, you may find that you're already meeting some of them really well, but that there are others that you're not handling so well. If you see a need for change, give yourself a pat on the back – the decision to improve your parenting is a cause for celebration. Your children will learn far more from watching you bravely struggle to create change than they ever would if things were 'perfect' from the start – just as they learn far more when we support them in their choices rather than choosing for them.

I have seen these strategies work well in many different settings (homes, hospitals, prisons, schools) with human beings of all ages (infants, toddlers, children, adolescents and adults) some of whom have had difficulties including autism, intellectual disability, ADHD, psychosis, mood disorders, anxiety disorders and relationship difficulties. But I have also seen these strategies abysmally fail to create the change wished for.

In many ways the strategies are the easy bit. What makes them work or not is your *approach* to their implementation. When it comes to creating change in children's emotions and behaviours, it is not *what* you do, but *how*. A strategy implemented in a playful, accepting and supportive way by an adult whose 'human' brain is switched on is always going to be more effective and helpful in the long run for learning and behaviour change than the same strategy implemented in a serious, judgemental and controlling way by a parent whose 'reptile brain' is activated.

In my experience, the following five approaches help to ensure that the strategies are more likely to succeed.

A PLAYFUL APPROACH

Listening to the sounds of children playing and laughing is one of the joys of parenting. Their chuckles, chattering and shrieks of delight tell us that all is well. To us, play may seem like a light-hearted endeavour – the 'opposite' of work – but for children playing *is* their work. Through play our children try out new ideas, attempt new tasks and practise relationships. In this way they are gradually developing their skills, confidence and resilience.

Next time your child is playing, take a moment to observe what he is doing (preferably when he can't see you). You'll often notice that he doesn't play in just one way, but will be flexible and try multiple versions of the same activity in different ways and with different outcomes. The development of a new skill through play means that when he makes mistakes it's not 'serious' ('We're just playing!'), and he won't feel ashamed at having made a mistake, as in true play there are no mistakes – just different ways of giving something a go. Playfulness is truly the antidote for seriousness and shame.

Sam and Jakob

Sam and Jakob, both toddlers, were making individual towers from building blocks. They put their blocks one on top of the other in various ways, trying different numbers of blocks, sometimes carefully, sometimes rapidly, sometimes straight, sometimes crooked, and eventually their towers fell over.

Sam was playing, so his crash was met with delight and pleasure. The fall didn't matter as it was part of the game. He simply collected up the blocks and tried again, building his skills, his confidence and his self-esteem: 'I can do it!'

But for Jakob, the tower building was 'serious', and his crash was met with distress and anger. The tower had not gone 'right' and didn't do what it was meant to. He blamed the blocks and cast them aside, stomping away. Opportunities for learning ended and Jakob was left feeling disappointed and angry.

Providing an atmosphere of playfulness in your family is one of the most important gifts you can give to your child. Playfulness is a state of being 'open to possibility', where different ways of doing, thinking or feeling are explored without fear or shame. So playfulness always involves possibilities and initiating action, and learning from this, which is why watching TV cannot be considered playful. Computer games can be playful, but they are typically quite limited in the possibilities available and allow little initiation. Often a player simply reacts to a scenario that is presented. That does not mean computer games should be banned, as they are an enormous amount of fun, and playing with friends (introducing the human element) can convert a simplistic game into a more complicated and playful experience.

The opposite of playfulness is seriousness – a 'closed' and inflexible state where only one way of doing, thinking or feeling is possible. Seriousness can be useful for tasks which really *must* be done a certain way, such as safely crossing a road, never playing with power points or wearing a seatbelt in the car.

However, when overused, seriousness can cause problems:

- If new skills and experiences are always 'serious', your child doesn't get to play, to try different options, and only learns what *you* think about these options rather than discovering what she thinks about them.
- Your child will always make mistakes when he tries to do something new. If there is only one way (and by implication one standard of achievement), then not meeting that standard will result in her feeling ashamed because she has failed. The emotions associated with shame are often quite intense and include anxiety, sadness and anger.
- The fear of being shamed for failing can inhibit her attempts at initiating and acquiring other new skills.

Obviously, playfulness and seriousness must be kept in balance. But in my experience of high-expectation families, the balance is often weighted too heavily towards seriousness. If in doubt, try to be flexible and find the fun in a situation. Children learn best in an environment free of criticism, judgement, measuring and perfectionism. In such a playful place, new things can be attempted and mistakes freely made without the fear of shame that so inhibits learning. There is still measuring and guiding – all parents need to guide their children – but it is done in a playful and accepting way.

If you find you are telling your children what to do, you are probably saving them and taking a serious approach. If you are letting your children try something out *their* way, you are probably supporting them and taking a playful approach. And if you want your strategies to not only work but also help your children to learn for themselves, avoid excessive seriousness.

Sarah and Maisie

Five-year-old Maisie was drawing in my room while I was talking with her mother, Sarah. Sarah tended to take a serious approach to parenting, mirroring her own childhood experience of being strictly disciplined and often feeling she didn't measure up to her parents' expectations. To her distress, Sarah found she tended to immediately find fault in her own daughter and this had led to many arguments and her experiencing a sense of misery and disappointment.

I asked Sarah to look at Maisie's drawing (which was missing a few things) and to imagine what her own mother would have said to her if it had been her drawing, and how this would have made her feel.

'She would have said something like, "That's nice, honey, but where are the ears and nose? And do you really think that a pink dress would look good with red hair?" And I would have felt not good enough, and wanted to scream at her, but I would never have dared. And it's silly, but I find myself saying the same things to Maisie.'

When we both stopped laughing at the ridiculousness of such negative comments on a five-year-old's drawing, I asked her what she would have wished her mother had said to her instead. To which she replied, 'Darling, what a wonderful drawing! Can I join in and draw as well?'

I replied, 'Why don't you say that to Maisie?'

Maisie beamed as her mother praised her, asked her if she could join in, and began drawing with her on the floor. (And Maisie added the nose when she saw her mother's drawing – but not the ears!)

Encouraging playfulness

One way of injecting playfulness into your family life is to have a regular game time. This can be as simple as playing catch with a soft ball, 'shopkeepers' (with very young children), backyard cricket, cards, board games, charades, singing, playing instruments, creating something, drawing, puzzles, footy, chess, computer games where players interact, water fights, holidays ... in fact anything where your family comes together with no point but the wish to enjoy each other's company.

Game time is useful for many reasons:

- It can be great fun.
- It creates connections and shared experiences between family members.
- It allows children to deal with the tensions and challenges of relationships (e.g. who goes first, sharing, fairness, competitiveness, control, disappointment, winning, losing, boasting, honesty, cheating, lying and truthfulness) in a playful environment. 'It's just a game', allows the tricky emotions associated with winning and losing to be explored. Parents can help keep the seriousness at bay, which always assists the negotiation of these emotions.

If you choose to have family games, it's best to start small with, say, a short (five minute) game of cards that involves more luck than skill such as Go Fish or Uno. Do this regularly and then gradually increase the time you spend together.

Sometimes your child will reject her family and the game, but don't worry about this. Don't force her to play, just keep offering her a place at the table (or wherever the game is set). Playing is about having fun, so if she chooses not to participate and you force her to, the logical consequence is that she won't have fun with you. If you leave it up to her, and keep the game playful, open and light, she's sure to want to join in. Very few children can pass up the opportunity to beat a parent at something – the sense of achievement is just too delightful!

Sometimes particularly stubborn children will reject the game so strongly that their pride won't allow them to back down. In this case, it may be worth trying to find a face-saving way out for them to re-enter the game at some point. If you keep offering a spot every now and again, and the players keep the game light, fun and free of shame, most children will be drawn back to the game.

What if the game gets serious?

A playful game can quickly turn serious if a child becomes angry or distressed when he is not winning and begins crying, cheating, or teasing other family members. This can lead to conflict and stress for everyone. Now this will probably sound odd, but bear with me. Rather than *react* to your child's negative emotions and behaviours, quietly celebrate this as an opportunity. If your child can't have fun playing a game, he is showing you that he is struggling with relationships and emotions. This becomes a wonderful opportunity for you to 'watch, wait and wonder' and to 'emotion coach' your child (see 'Attunement' on page 29). It indicates how important it is for you and your children to *keep* playing regularly together so that they can discover ways of getting over the emotions that relationships bring up.

So, *watch* what is happening, *wait* (don't react) and *wonder* 'What is going on for my child?'

Once you are aware of the emotion, use it is an opportunity for intimacy and learning. Listen to your child's feelings and perhaps share with him an example when you felt like cheating, lying or teasing. Then help your child find the words to name the emotion they are feeling and to understand where it came from. And finally, gently but firmly set limits around the game, and work out how the problem can be solved or the conflict be repaired.

A SUPPORTIVE APPROACH

As explained in Part 1, when our children are babies they depend on us because they are unable to understand their problems, let alone sort them out. At this age, when they have a problem we step in, decide what needs to be done for them and do it – we 'save' them. In doing so we take on the responsibility for the problem, and our children learn and expect that if they have a problem, the way to fix it is to get a parent to take over.

When our children are independent adults (able to parent themselves), they are able to understand and sort out their own problems. At this time we don't step in, tell them what to do, or decide for them – we support them as they handle the problem themselves. If they ask, we may make ourselves available to work on the problem with them (affiliation), but the difficulty remains the responsibility of our adult children. When a problem afflicts an adult child who is supported, there is no expectation of the parent being able to solve it, and no disappointment and anger with the parent if the problem is unable to be solved.

Promoting the move from dependence to independence requires a shift in our approach to our child. With infants the approach is low support and high saving, and with teenagers it is high support and low saving. Thus as our children grow, there will be a slow but steady change in the balance between supporting and saving. In any situation where there is the option of either approach, it is generally better to err on the side of supporting. Though there is a risk that they may make an unhelpful decision (though this experience also provides an opportunity for learning), the gain is that they will increasingly develop the belief that they are competent, can trust themselves and take responsibility for their own thoughts and actions.

Saving our children may allay our own anxieties about harm coming to them, but every time we do it we are treating them like infants, and giving them the message, 'I don't think you are capable of thinking about, understanding or choosing wisely in this situation.'

Now of course there are times when we do need to save our children by telling them what to do or preventing them from doing what they want. Boundaries are very important (see Chapter 9), and if our child were in danger we would step in and save them. I am certainly not advocating a 'hands off' approach to parenting while they are dependent – just more of a supportive approach wherever possible. However, it's crucial to realise that excessively saving your child limits the development of confidence, competence and personal responsibility.

Sometimes, however, the habit of saving is so ingrained in us that we are not even aware that we are doing it. Here's what you might say if you were saving an upset or distressed child or adolescent:

- 'You didn't need that friend anyway.'
- 'Don't be such a sook.'
- 'Well you need to study harder.'
- 'You must have done something to make him angry at you.'
- 'Stop thinking so negatively.'

Each of these responses is telling them what to think or do – effectively saying, 'I know best and you can't deal with it.'

On the other hand, this is what you might say if you were supporting them:

- 'I'm so sorry, honey. It must've been awful to read that text.'
- 'I'm here if you need me.'
- 'Is there anything you'd like me to do?'
- 'Would you mind if I gave you a hug?'
- 'What are you going to do now?'
- 'I wonder why it all went so wrong.'

Each of these responses is effectively saying, 'I'm on your side; I believe you can work it out and I'm here to help if you need me.'

Saving and supporting at a funeral

Most of us have attended a funeral with a friend who has lost someone dear to them. The emotions are raw and intense. We can see they are suffering, and the emotional wish in ourselves to stop their suffering is strong. Many of us think, 'I don't know what to say.' This is because in times of grief a person's mammalian brain is suffering from a sudden loss of connection, so their human brain is not working well and they actually *can't* think of anything to say.

However, instead of sitting with this (watching, waiting and listening), well-meaning people try to save their friend from their grief:

- 'Don't cry.'
- 'Have a good cry.'

- 'She's in a better place now.'
- 'It's all for the best.'
- 'Let's go get a few drinks.'
- 'Take these sleeping tablets.'

The grieving person is being told what to do, think or feel – advice that is directed at their human brain which, of course, is no longer working properly. Instead, their mammalian brain is in charge, and it simply wants to feel connected with others in their grief.

By far the better approach is to support them:

- Say, 'I'm so sorry for your loss.'
- Give them a hug, make eye contact, stand close, and simply share the experience with them, accepting whatever emotions come up.
- Listen when your friend starts to talk about their loved one (don't start banging on about your own experiences of death/funerals unless they ask – which is unlikely as they will be submerged in their own grief).
- Offer yourself, 'I'm always here.'
- Gently ask questions if it feels appropriate.

A REPAIRING APPROACH

We all make mistakes. As we get better at something we make less mistakes, but no matter how good we get, no one is perfect. One of the skills our children need to learn is how to fix things up after they go wrong, particularly within relationships.

If a child's experience is that messing up (and its attendant disappointment expressed as strong emotion) is generally followed by the problem being repaired (and the relationship remaining supportive and loving), then she develops the confidence to give new things a go. There is no fear or excessive shame in making mistakes because she trusts that things can be fixed and that she will still be loved.

A child feels safe to be angry at his mother for saying no to a request, because after the conflict there is repair through forgiveness, hugs and an ability to talk about what happened. This helps him to get over his disappointment and to change his expectations. He can also allow himself to feel deeply sad, because he has learned through experience that the sadness passes.

Through the experience of mistakes and strong emotions being 'fixed', children learn that there is no need to fear either making a mistake or strong emotions, and they will try new things.

However, if children experience that mistakes or strong emotions result in shame, disappointment and a disruption in the relationship with their parent, then making mistakes or having strong emotions are experienced as very dangerous. Such children may become perfectionists, which stunts their ability to give things a go or results in the need to excessively control. Or they avoid strong emotions such as anger or sadness. Or they feel the emotions but get stuck in them; holding grudges with rage, or experiencing the hopelessness of a sadness that does not seem to pass.

Amy

Seven-year-old Amy was not happy. Her mother had just had a baby and had been in hospital with the newborn for the past three days. Amy and her older sister had been cared for variously by her father, the grandparents and family friends, and had been in every day to see her mother. But on the third night her father found her curled in a ball in the corner of her room crying. When he tried to comfort her, she yelled 'Go away!' and hit him. He didn't react and simply stayed with her, asking what was wrong. The anger passed and she began crying harder – tears flowing down her face – and said in a 'baby' voice 'I want Mamma home.' Amy had missed out and felt it strongly with both anger and sadness.

Her father said, 'You seem to be very angry and sad all at the same time. Would you like to talk to Mum?'

Initially, Amy angrily said 'No!', but the father simply waited and asked the same thing in a different way. After a few moments Amy nodded her head.

The phone call was difficult for Amy. She said little as the father explained briefly to Amy's mother what had happened. Amy's mother was able to say how hard it must be for Amy to be away from her for three days, but how when Amy was a new baby (like her baby brother was now) she could hardly be away from her mother for three minutes. She said she would see Amy in the morning and that she was coming home in two days. Amy didn't respond, but her tears had stopped. When she was asked if she'd like to fall asleep on her mum's side of the bed, Amy said she would and by the end of the call she was smiling and gave her dad a big hug. With prompting she was also able to say sorry for hitting her father.

Amy had missed out and was angry and sad, but her father and mother were able to help fix it by not reacting, wondering with Amy what was wrong, and helping her feel that although she wasn't with her mother, she was still important. So there was an emotional repair and reconnection – not exactly what Amy wanted, but near enough. And there was also a logical repair, with ideas like the baby needing more time than Amy at the moment, Amy would see her mother in a few hours, her mother would be home in a couple of days, and Amy being able to fall asleep in her mother's spot that night.

The first part in taking a repairing approach is to view mistakes and strong emotions as positive things: to be able to say to yourself, 'My child *needs* to make mistakes, and he *needs* to experience the strong emotions associated with missing out.' This is your 'human' brain kicking in (of course, if you are in reptile mode and feeling overwhelmed by your own feelings, you won't even be able to think about repairing).

Once you feel calm and thoughtful you can help your child's reptilian brain become calmer. By showing your child care and focusing on recharging his attachment battery you help his mammalian brain feel cared for and connected. This is the emotional and relational repair: he was feeling disconnected through the shame of a mistake or the emotions of grief or disappointment, and through your or his actions he felt reconnected. Once his reptilian brain is soothed and his mammal brain is secured, then the final stage of repair can occur.

Using his human brain your child can work with you to make

sense of what happened using words and ideas. You talk about the mistake that occurred using a story, or you name the emotions that he was feeling, or you discuss actions that can be taken to physically help the situation. The cost or consequence of the mistake is then addressed, but always remembering that you are trying to help your child feel cared for before you correct him. And finally, you and/or your child put the emotional experience of repair into words by saying sorry. It doesn't have to happen straight away, but it does have to happen. And the best way to encourage it is to model it whenever possible.

AN EXPERIENCED APPROACH

Actions speak louder than words. When it comes to emotions and relationships, words have a weak effect when compared to experience. You can tell your child one hundred times that she needs to 'calm down' or 'be more considerate', but often this just leaves her feeling shamed that she is not measuring up to what you expect.

A far more powerful approach is for her to experience you being calm and considerate with her. You can tell her not to smoke or swear, but these will be wasted words if you smoke or swear. You can tell her to get over her disappointment, but it will have little effect on how she manages missing out if your own approach to disappointment is unmanageable rage.

As I have explained repeatedly, if you want your child to behave in a particular way, there is no substitute for you modelling what you wish for. Though we may see the problem and solution for our children, there is little point in saying anything if it is not strongly backed up by our own behaviour.

A COOPERATIVE APPROACH

In Chapter 3 I talked about how our reptilian brain's focus on survival is such a powerful influence on our behaviour and relationships. Because its primary concern is to prevail, there is an instinctive (and often unconscious) drive to compete with others and to either dominate and control, or submit and exit (fight/flight). This means that when our children are feeling threatened or angry about something that has happened, say, at school, and they lash out at us, we often become defensive and immediately want to resist or fight whatever is being aggressively sent our way. Our human brains know that our children's behaviour is not personal, and that they just need practice and guidance in handling strong emotions, but our reptilian brain senses a threat and its instantaneous response is to try to 'win'. This need to win (as opposed to lose) is a major problem when it comes to relationships. I know of many families where a parent's need to win leads to endless competition with the children (and the other partner), creating a tense and ultimately destructive family dynamic.

The alternative to reptilian competing is to take a cooperative approach – something only our mammalian and human brains are capable of. When someone is attempting to dominate us, we don't get caught up in the competition (win–lose). We do not resist or defend against their aggression, but instead accept that it is happening, and try to cooperate with them (win–win). In this way we leave the problem-solving to a later time when emotions are not running so high.

If a child in 'lizard mode' is trying to dominate and win (either physically or verbally), rather than us trying to resist them (which generally escalates tension and aggression), we can take a non-resistant approach. For example, if your child angrily grabs your arm with both hands and tries to pull you in a certain direction and you resist by pulling back, the child will usually pull harder and a tug-of-war will ensue until someone gives in. A non-resistant approach is to allow your arm to relax and simply go where your child is taking you, saying something like, 'You want to go this way? Okay, off we go.' When the 'grabber' meets with no resistance, the tension drops and it's hard for them to maintain their aggression – you have turned a potentially competitive interaction into a cooperative one.

It is important to note that non-resistance is not submission – you are simply not joining in the competition the other person has set up. It doesn't mean you remain passive if your children's behaviour puts them or others in acute danger – this is a 'lose–lose' situation. In such cases you may have to step in and save them by giving direct advice, shepherding them away from danger, or taking hold of them until they calm down.

If your children's dominating behaviour is verbal, you simply listen and do not argue the point with them. In the face of strong emotion, never defend yourself: it is a waste of breath and increases tension and suffering for almost no benefit. Whatever the issue, it will always be better to discuss it at a later time when everyone is thinking clearly. 'When we've all calmed down we can work it out together.' As I've previously stated, confidence is everything, and being confident that we are 'good enough' parents allows us to accept our children's accusations without needing to defend ourselves.

Parents who use a cooperative and accepting approach with their children and with each other will foster healthier and happier family dynamics. There is a great deal of wisdom in the old saying: 'Do you want to be right, or do you want to be happy?'

CHAPTER 5

PROVIDE ENOUGH SAFETY

It was Abraham Maslow who suggested that though humans had various needs, some were more important than others. His influential idea was that you couldn't meet the more complex needs of humans until their more basic ones were met, which became known as Maslow's Hierarchy. Voltaire expressed similar sentiments when he stated, 'Feed men, then ask for virtue.'

Other than the obvious preconditions for life such as food, water and oxygen, safety is the bedrock need of our children, and this is why I place it as the number one thing that children need us to provide. It is why with children at risk of suicide, deliberate self-harm, anorexia nervosa or drug abuse, the first task along with a thorough psychological assessment is to develop a risk management plan. I've found that neither the child nor the parents tend to be able to concentrate on psychological work until there is a sense that both the child and his family are safe enough. Without safety, we don't tend to reflect thoughtfully, we react emotionally.

As we have seen, attachment theory suggests that children's primary drive is to feel safe, and that they will feel safe and secure when they believe that they are on our minds enough. However, children will also feel insecure if the person they are attached to (their protector) is themselves unsafe i.e. scared or uncertain. When I work with children who have witnessed domestic violence, many are more messed up about seeing their mother hurt than being hurt themselves. Strategies to help our children feel secure will have little impact if there are actual dangers in their lives or in ours. Thus:

- The abuse of the child or anyone in the child's life must be stopped immediately and totally, so the child experiences and eventually believes she and her loved ones are safe enough.
- The adults in the child's life must get whatever help is required to be as physically and mentally healthy as possible, and as unaffected by substances as possible. The child needs to believe and experience that his loved ones will be present, available, thoughtful and caring of him.
- The adults must move towards decreasing actual dangers in the child's environment, so the child genuinely believes she and her family are safe. This may involve, for example, getting an intervention order, contacting the police or child protection services, even moving house away from a dangerous environment – whatever it takes.

If the actual dangers in a child's life cannot be resolved despite all attempts at doing 'whatever it takes', the child is likely to feel chronically insecure, with all of the emotional and social problems that such insecurity brings. Of course, no child can be perfectly safe at all times. There are some dangers that cannot be minimised by any intervention, and include things like:

- An unexpected injury or illness that cannot be healed or managed adequately
- An unexpected death
- Accidents and natural events
- The unpredictable actions of others (abuse; criminal or dangerous acts).

If we or our children are unlucky enough to experience a random, accidental unsafe event that cannot be resolved, our task is to grieve with them for both the event itself, and for the uncertainty and fragility of life. This means moving through denial, bargaining, anger and sadness about the event, and in the end accepting that there are no guarantees, that bad things can happen to good people, and that though the world can be full of joy, it can also be a very sad place – as one mother said to me, 'Be happy when it's happy, and sad when it's sad.'

Jason

Ten-year-old Jason lived with his mother. Though a capable and well-liked student, he was refusing to attend school, complaining of multiple aches and pains for which no cause could be found despite numerous investigations and visits to medical professionals with his mother. Before he saw me, many unsuccessful attempts had been made to get him back to school, including anxiety management and behavioural strategies.

In the first session with Jason and his mother it came up that his parents had separated two years previously. When I asked his mother how she had coped with this loss physically and mentally, I noted Jason become still. She seemed somewhat flat, but said (unconvincingly) that she was doing 'okay'. Later I asked Jason to go back to the waiting room, and when I asked again how she was doing she admitted to experiencing a depressed mood and suicidal thoughts since her partner left. She also described a suicide attempt shortly after the separation that left her in hospital overnight when Jason was staying with his father. She was adamant that Jason didn't know about this or how she felt because she put on a brave face during the day and only cried alone at night. I told her that there was every chance that he had picked up on her low mood, and I obtained permission to share with Jason my observation that she seemed flat.

Jason was brought back in and I commented that his mum seemed a bit sad. I asked how he thought his mother was doing. He was nervous to answer this and it took some time, but to his great credit he bravely (and through tears) divulged that he thought she was sad a lot. He also said that a cousin had told him ('though you're not meant to know so don't say anything') that she had even tried to kill herself last year. He hated going to school because he worried he'd come home and she would be dead – he was staying home to keep her alive.

Jason's mother was shocked to learn that he knew this, and to their credit, the two of them were able to talk about his fears for her safety. She was able to commit to getting help, told him she had only taken an overdose once shortly after the separation, and promised that she would never try to harm herself again, making a safety plan that she signed in Jason's presence.

This was an enormous relief to Jason and helped him be convinced that she was safe enough to be left alone at home. As Jason's mother's depression lifted, Jason's physical symptoms abated, and he was able to go back to school.

When a child feels unsafe or overwhelmed by their emotions

If children or their loved ones are actually unsafe, our role as parents as outlined above is quite obvious – to remove the real danger.

But there are times where they *feel* unsafe, but they are actually quite safe. A few examples include:

- Separation anxiety
- A fear that there are monsters in their room at night
- A fear that something bad could happen to their parent.

At other times, intense and overwhelming feelings can also make a child feel insecure and unsafe. A few examples include:

- A child having a severe tantrum over 'missing out' on something and causing damage to people or property
- A young person sobbing and pulling at their hair or scratching themselves due to a relationship breakdown.

In all of these situations, there is no actual danger that you can remove. The problem is that the child feels highly emotional and insecure from a mixture of fear, anger and sadness, and they have stopped thinking clearly because the more primitive parts of their brain have taken over.

The first thing that needs to be done is to help your child soothe their survival brain and turn their thinking brain back on. Talking will have little effect until they are soothed. Eventually we hope they will be able to soothe themselves, but until then, we can support our child's self-soothing by responding in a calm, reasonable and predictable way (not always easy when emotions are high and accusations flying). This is where the four-stage plan comes in very handy.

THE FOUR-STAGE PLAN

As we saw in Chapter 3, fear is an important trigger for action when we are in immediate physical danger (the fight/flight response), but when the perceived danger is imagined or fear stops us from thinking, it makes us react and not reflect, and can lead to aggression and other unhelpful responses.

The least helpful response you can give to a terrified child who is sobbing or acting out is to escalate the problem by becoming angry or sad yourself. Next on the list of what not to do is to freeze up with uncertainty: 'What do I do now?' Having a clear plan that you and the other adults in your child's life can predictably follow helps the adults stay calmer and clearer about what to do, and models that crises *can* be managed.

The core idea of the plan is that it is much better to support children as they resolve their own problems than to step in and save them by telling them what to do. This means you need to view a child's problem as *their* problem, not *your* problem, and avoid taking responsibility (saving them) unless you absolutely have to.

The stages are as follows:

1. Allow your child to sort it out herself.
2. Observe your child quietly while she sorts out her problem.
3. Offer some advice to help her deal with the problem.
4. Step in and sort it out by telling her what to do (or if necessary enlist support from mental health services or emergency services).

Stage 1: Allow your child to sort it out

A trap we can all fall into is that when we see a problem that has temporarily overwhelmed our child, we immediately try to fix it. However, as we have seen, this not only gives the child the message that we don't believe he is competent to manage it himself but also does not allow him to practise his own emotion regulation and problem-solving skills. Even though in the end you might have to step in and save him, it is important that you go through the process of supporting him first so he has to initiate an action and learn from this, which helps in developing competence and resilience. The support process is as follows:

- **Recognise** that a crisis is happening for your child, and that she is overwhelmed. (This sounds obvious, but some parents are reluctant to acknowledge the depth of their child's emotions and will play down the situation to avoid dealing with their own unresolved feelings.)
- **Name** her problem and/or emotion (e.g. 'I wonder if you're feeling angry about what happened at school today', 'I get the feeling that you are a bit stressed by your homework', 'You don't seem to be getting on very well this afternoon').
- **Support** her by confirming that you believe she can sort out her own problem ('I reckon you can give this a good go', 'I think you can sort out who gets to play first').
- **Give her a time limit** ('I'll come back in one/five/ten minutes to see how you are doing').

The time limit is important, because it puts some boundaries around the problem, effectively saying, 'This situation won't go on forever, so why not have a go at ending it yourself?' Remember to use few words and repeat yourself rather than engage in an emotion-laden discussion. (Obviously, if a child's life or health is in danger, you must skip the support stages and jump straight to saving. For example, you wouldn't take a supportive approach to a toddler who was wandering towards a busy road; you would save them by grabbing their arm and telling them what to do. And you wouldn't take a supportive approach to a young person who was about to take an overdose. You would step in and take the tablets away from them and seek professional assistance.)

Stage 2: Observe your child while he sorts it out

If your child hasn't managed to solve his problem after the time limit in Stage 1, it's time to move onto the next stage:

- Name the problem again, and tell him that you still believe he can manage it.
- This time, though, stay with him while he tries to solve it. You don't give advice, you are simply with him. You also give him a time limit, 'I'll sit here with you for one/five/ten minutes while you try to sort it out' (e.g. deciding who will play computer first, doing homework, completing a household chore).
- When he tries to get you to step in, stay calm and reassure him that he can do it: 'It's okay. I'm staying out of it for now. You can work it out I'm sure.'

It may be (especially with older children) that your offer to quietly be with them is rejected and they tell you to go away. That is absolutely fine. You are not trying to save them at this stage, just offering them your support. If they reject this support, you can simply compromise your withdrawal ('I'll just wait out here while you sort it out. I'll come and see you in five/ten minutes to see how you are going'). You won't barge into their space without asking, but you let them know that you are willing to be with them at this tricky time.

From an attachment perspective, your non-intrusive presence and them being on your mind may help them feel more secure and may help them to start thinking and reflecting again. This non-intrusive presence is a hard step for some parents whose typical approach is to play director, and may also be hard for the children of such parents as they are waiting and expecting to be reprimanded and told what to do. It can take a lot of practice for some parents to simply be with their children without taking a leading role. Playing games, watching

TV, walking or driving together in calm silence (at least from your perspective) are all good ways of practising simply being together, and can help at those times when things are far from calm.

Stage 3: Offer some advice

If the problem is still overwhelming ask permission to try to help – again with a time limit: 'Would you like me to see if I can help for five/ten minutes?'

If the answer is 'yes', you could offer to go and get a drink of water, bring in a beanbag and blanket, take them to their 'bolt-hole' (see 'Soothing the Reptilian Brain' on page 74), get them a lollipop, give them a hug, or offer to go for a walk with them. You are not telling them what to do, or how to do it, just offering suggestions that they can accept or reject – the final decision is still theirs.

If their answer is 'no', then that is okay, but the time limit still stands and if the problem is not resolved and their emotions aren't soothed by the end of that time, you'll move to the final stage.

Stage 4: Step in and sort it out

At this point you need to tell your child, 'You did your best but I'm going to help you now with your problem.' (Even at this final stage, you want to keep it clear that the problem is not yours but his).

- Tell your child what he needs to do to feel safe and soothed again.
- Enlist support from the other parent. At this stage you just have to keep going as a parenting unit, doing whatever it takes until the crisis is resolved, and in most situations your family's resources will be enough.

However, sometimes despite the best efforts of your child and your family, you may not be able to diminish the crisis and its risk (I'm thinking here of depression, eating disorders or extreme risk-taking such as drug abuse and criminal activity). In general, if your child is unable to cope with his problems and emotions, you and your partner are feeling overwhelmed and your family's resources are stretched to the limit, you should not just sit with the uncertainty and anxiety – it is time to get more help.

It is beyond the scope of this book to discuss how you would deal with such situations, but it is likely to involve your family, a mental health response and possibly even a police, emergency or legal response. You need to keep working at it until you are not scared anymore and are confident you have done everything you can to help your family. Working with a professional can help you obtain that confidence.

It is your children's repeated experiences that overwhelming emotions can be handled, problems can be solved, insecurities soothed, and sense made of their world that helps develop their optimism, confidence and competence. If we go to Stage 4 too quickly, we may solve an immediate problem, but we prevent our children from learning for themselves, and may leave them feeling less rather than more competent.

CHAPTER 6

PROVIDE FOR THEIR BASIC NEEDS

As we saw in the previous chapter, along with obvious physical needs for food, water and shelter, feeling safe is the most crucial for children's development. When children are safe enough, you can then move to consider other needs:

- Do they have enough nutritious food and adequate exercise?
- Do they have optimal medical treatment for any physical or mental illnesses?
- Are they are attending a school that meets their educational and social needs?
- Do they have enough ritual and routine in their life, especially around sleeping?
- Are they broadly connected within their community?
- Do they have a healthy balance of activity and boredom?
- Do they hear 'no' and miss out enough so they can get angry and then learn how to get over it? (See Chapter 9.)
- Are they prevented from experiencing adult activities prematurely?

The first three needs are obvious and require little in the way of explanation. However, some people are surprised that I place ritual and routine among children's basic needs, others don't grasp the importance of being broadly connected within their community, and many children and teenagers would be surprised (and possibly annoyed) that I list boredom, missing out and not entering adulthood prematurely as basic needs.

Connor

Eight-year-old Connor had been at a school for four months when his school contacted me. He was always getting into trouble because of inattention, hyperactivity and disruptive behaviour, and often turned up late without any lunch and dressed in dirty, ragged clothing. Despite numerous attempts over that time to discuss the school's concerns with his parents, meetings were not attended and there was a sense of hopelessness about how to help him. The school wondered if he might have attention deficit hyperactivity disorder (ADHD), and asked me to assess whether medication may be helpful.

I arranged to see the school and the parents, which was important because even if I diagnosed ADHD, medication is not adequate unless it is used safely, appropriately and as part of a package of change including parent work.

The parents did not attend despite the school's insistence. It became obvious that the issue for Connor was one of parental neglect in multiple areas: he was hungry, his clothing was substandard, he wasn't provided with adequate schooling materials, and numerous requests for Connor's mental health to be assessed went unheeded despite his distress and dysfunction academically and socially.

The school had used all their resources to effect a change for Connor, and it was decided the only course of action left was to involve child protection to assess the family and ensure the boy's basic needs were met. This was to include a mental health assessment around Connor's disruptive behaviour and whether he may have had a formal psychiatric diagnosis such as ADHD.

Unfortunately, this story does not have a happy ending. The family were seen once by protective workers and agreements reached, but when child protection returned to the home the family had vanished. It is uncertain what happened to Connor, except to say that it was unlikely things would have improved for him while his basic needs went unmet.

THE NEED FOR RITUAL, ROUTINE AND REPETITION

Ritual provides children with a sense of control – being able to predict what will happen next even when they may not understand the whole situation. Routine gives them a sense of security and is experienced as comforting at both a logical (human brain) and an emotional (mammal brain) level, the latter being where repeated experience has the greatest effect. Of course, too *much* ritual can be experienced as controlling and stifling of growth and initiative, so it is about having the right balance.

Reflect on your children's world and how predictable it is:

- When and how do they wake up?
- What happens between waking and getting to school? (Schools tend to do ritual well – think of the school bell, break times, the timetable, the uniform, the rules etc.)
- What happens between school ending and dinnertime?
- What happens at dinner? (When, how, what and with whom do they eat?)
- What happens after dinner up until bedtime?
- What is the ritual around bedtime and sleep?
- What happens to the routine on weekends?
- If your child lives in two separate houses, what is the ritual around leaving one household and entering the other?
- What are the rituals around school holidays?
- What is the ritual around any physical affection?
- What 'family time' rituals do you have? (E.g. Do you provide a brief regular family time where any family issues can be discussed? Do you regularly get together as a family to play games or be playful together? Or at least eat together?)

In all of these rituals and routines, the important factor is repetition, repetition, repetition! This is because our children's emotional brains learn best through repeated experiences. Repetition is required to learn all skills whether they be physical, intellectual, social or emotional – how to fall asleep, how to walk, how to read, how to play an instrument, how to be hygienic, how to deal with being left out, and how to cope with disappointment, just to name a few.

If your child is developing slowly in an emotional or relationship area or has some habits that aren't helpful, I'm not going to beat about the bush: you and your partner need to take a big breath and say to yourselves, 'Change is going to take a *long* time.'

If for thirteen years your child has coped with relationship tension by nagging and being oppositional, changing this approach is not going to take thirteen hours or even thirteen weeks but more like thirteen months. So whatever change you are hoping to make, it needs to be repeated again, and again, and *again*. This is the only way that your child's brain will stop trying to use the old patterns and use the new ones instead.

But it is important to remember that as you and your child start to do new things, the old ways will still make appearances. Just as you think you and your child are consistently doing the new thing you hope for, out pops the old way. When this happens, it is vital to put the problem in context and remember that change *has* occurred (even if it feels like you are taking one step forward and two steps back).

The value of music and movement

Most cultures incorporate music and movement within their rituals. Dance, martial arts, singing and drumming not only help children to develop control over their bodies, but also help with emotion regulation by calming an agitated reptilian brain and connecting an insecure mammalian brain. If you have access to music or movement within your family or community, use it. Take any opportunity you have to sing with each other, even if it's only nursery rhymes, 'happy birthday' or your football club anthem. Shared music is one of the most connecting experiences a group can have.

As a family, it is vital that you get out of the house and move together. Walking, running, cycling and hiking are all simple and cheap ways of sharing experiences that use repetitive movement and are therefore potentially soothing as well as meeting attachment needs.

Bedtime and sleep

One of the most important routines is the one your family devises around bedtime. On school nights in particular, your child needs to go to sleep at a reasonable time. Children expend enormous amounts of energy learning, growing and moving, and sleep is essential for rest and repair. As a rough guide, young children need around eleven or twelve hours each night, and even upper primary school-aged children need at least nine or ten hours. Teenagers may insist they 'don't need sleep', but puberty is exhausting and many sleep up to twelve hours.

It is considered unwise to allow electronic equipment in your child's room other than music. My experience is that TVs, computers, mobile phones and electronic games put adolescent children at significant risk of sleep problems. Some may be able to handle these technologies in their room, but if there is any evidence of sleep difficulties, their removal would be the first step (with the secondary benefit of your child being told 'no' and missing out – see later in this chapter).

Good sleep habits

- No caffeine from any source after 4 p.m., or at all before puberty.
- Make sure any distractions are removed (you'd be surprised how many teenagers are texting their friends and waking them up in the middle of the night).
- No getting into bed for anything other than sleep or sexual activity. No eating, reading, watching TV or playing games. Sleep is a reptile brain activity. Don't confuse the reptile by doing things in bed that involve being alert.
- Get the best possible bed, bedding, pyjamas and room environment (not too cold or hot, no noise).

- Experience natural light as much as possible; opening the curtains upon waking helps to synchronise the sleep–wake body clock.
- Exercise during the day and try to get outside to see the horizon. Research has found that though running on a treadmill is good, running outside is much better for sleep and mental health.
- Don't nap during the day as it steals from your sleep at night.
- Wake up at the same time every school/work morning, and try to go to sleep at the same time every evening.
- If you can't fall asleep within thirty minutes, get up and do something quiet and boring for fifteen minutes and then try again.
- Add meditation, muscle relaxation and breathing exercises to the above.
- Try to lose weight if you are overweight, and try to stop smoking (nicotine is a stimulant).
- Don't use sleeping tablets, alcohol or marijuana to fall asleep. Any benefit is usually significantly outweighed by the cost.
- Treat any mental illness; almost all of them are associated with poor sleep.

THE NEED FOR COMMUNITY CONNECTIONS

It is important that you involve your child in the broader community. The more connections your child has with people and events outside your own extended family, the more they will feel part of the wider community. Connections are often made through sporting activities, but also through music and the arts (e.g. group singing) and membership of volunteer organisations or environmental groups. Nationalism, ethnic identity and religion are particularly powerful forms of community connection. They provide rituals, symbols, songs and shared cultural experiences that can act as a type of social glue. However for all their benefits, they can have a darker side. Group identities can also encourage unquestioned acceptance and obedience, and can subtly generate pressures to conform. If not handled carefully, they can also lead to a sense of 'us and them', with the potential for exclusion and intolerance.

As thoughtful and mature adults, we need to be aware of the pros and cons of these group identities, and to encourage our children to somewhat identify with groups, but also at an appropriate age to help them see that group identity can be problematic where it excludes others, limits tolerance, and inhibits freedom of thinking.

Support public institutions. Visiting the local park, pool or library, using public transport, attending community memorials and volunteering for tree plantings or cleanups are all ways to teach your children about community connections and to help them feel part of a safe community. It helps them get a sense that 'we're all in this together', and encourages the cohesiveness and goodwill necessary for a healthy society whose members look out for each other.

The more broadly connected your child is within their community and world, the safer and more secure they will feel. Ironically, the wish to protect our children by keeping them safe in the private realm can actually lead to our children feeling more insecure in their wider world.

THE NEED FOR BOREDOM

When children complain of boredom, many parents panic and rush to offer suggestions or, even worse, drop everything to try to entertain them. This does the child a great disservice. From a young age, children need to be given periods of time in which they have to play and initiate activities by themselves.

Coping with and tolerating boredom supports the development of self-assertion and self-confidence, individuation, mastery of one's own initiative, and imagination. Allowing our children to experience boredom communicates important messages:

- 'I am not at your beck-and-call.'
- 'This is your problem to sort out.'
- 'You can do this.'

On a practical level, it also gives you some time away from your children so you can charge your own batteries. Trying to relieve your child's boredom ('saving' them from their feelings) sets up an unhealthy dependency on you, and may inhibit development. By all means arrange activities that promote your child's growth and enjoyment, but just make sure that these are balanced with adequate time for your child to be bored so they initiate and discover things for themselves.

How much time you set aside for 'boredom' will depend on your child's age and temperament. 'Watch, wait and wonder' (see page 29) is a good way for you to support your child as they experience boredom and initiating. And if your child struggles in their own company, 'start low and go slow'– gradually exposing your child to the challenge of having to initiate for themselves. Also, before you give them time alone, it is helpful to charge up their 'attachment battery' (see page 22).

For older children, during these solo periods, do not allow them to use electronic media such as music, TV, mobile phones, computers or gaming consoles. Your child will be passively absorbing information or following instructions rather than genuinely creating and initiating their own ideas.

Of course, your child may not like being exposed to boredom, and will probably complain to a greater or lesser extent. You and your partner will need the confidence to be able to tolerate these attacks, and yet still hold the line: 'It is okay for you to be bored some of the time.'

You will need to model the same behaviour you expect of your child. If you constantly have the TV, radio or stereo on, or are surfing the net or texting friends at every opportunity then it is hypocritical to expect your child to put up with boredom.

THE NEED TO MISS OUT

While it might feel counterintuitive in our indulgent and hovering parenting culture, it is vital that your child is regularly and confidently told 'no' and misses out. As we saw in Chapter 2, children at an emotional and subconscious level absurdly expect everything from their parents, and since it is impossible to avoid disappointing them, they are bound to feel anger or hatred towards us at times throughout their development. You will not have to manufacture or create opportunities for missing out – they will happen quite naturally.

The way children get over their absurd expectations and develop more realistic ones is to feel their disappointment and rage at being unable to get what they want – to truly experience the grief and loss – and come to accept that while they don't get *everything* they want, they get *enough*. By you gently, firmly and confidently helping your child to miss out, they also learn that while they are wonderful and loved, they are not special. It is actually a great help for your child to know that they cannot break down your resolve through emotional outbursts, as it helps them come to a more rapid acceptance of missing out. If your child knows that you will give in occasionally, they may not modify their expectations to a more reasonable level. It is hard for a child to accept missing out if in the past they were able to get what they wanted by ramping up their whining or rage. By giving in, you are making it harder for yourself and for them.

It is through *repeatedly* facing and 'getting over' disappointment that a child gradually learns to change their expectations. Avoiding or 'moving on' from disappointment simply puts it off to a later time (see 'Getting over Grief and Hate' on page 61). It is better to experience a child's disappointment and rage as a toddler or child than as a teenager or young adult.

When helping a child face disappointment, avoid a harsh, defensive, or dismissive approach ('Build a bridge and get over it!' was one mother's unfortunate response to her child's complaints). Taking a playful, accepting and supportive approach (as described in Chapter 4) is a good start.

However, if confidence is the problem, try practising saying 'no' into a mirror. Unity with your partner is also vital (see page 127), since one firm parent is of no use if the other parent caves in – your child will not only maintain their absurd expectations but also their attempts at breaking down your resolve, putting further strain on your relationship.

THE NEED TO AVOID PREMATURE ADULT EXPERIENCES

Experimentation with alcohol, cigarettes, drugs, gambling and sex is a normal developmental phase for most adolescents and young adults. It would be foolish for a parent to think that their child would not at some point come into contact with these experiences. However, the dangers of such experimentation can seem very scary to parents, especially when their adolescent's thinking brain is hamstrung by powerful needs to belong to their peer group and by see-sawing emotions, and the fact that they are increasingly spending time away from the safety of home. Indeed, research clearly shows that the younger a person is when they engage in these activities, the worse the outcome for their mental and physical wellbeing in adulthood. Conversely, the longer they delay experimentation with these activities, the better the outcome.

Guiding your child away from premature adult experiences is best managed with a mixture of openness and understanding, and clear boundaries that both parents (and the young person if possible) agree to and are comfortable with. Try to do this without your home becoming like a police station, but also not simply agreeing to whatever your young person wants. You need to be confident that you are being reasonable. (See Chapter 9 for tips on negotiating boundaries.)

You have a central role in guiding your children and protecting them from harm, but as they mature, this role changes to supporting them more and saving them less. Children are a wondrous uncertainty, and they are not you. In the end they will have to decide for themselves what they will and will not do, and your parental role is to gradually prepare them for this. Taking an authoritarian 'I said so' approach of do's and don'ts may keep them safe while they are with you, but may leave them more vulnerable as they increasingly spend more time away from you. Sometimes you have to take a short-term risk to achieve a long-term gain.

Though each family and home is unique, there are some basic rules or standards that provide a starting point for discussion. Some will be non-negotiable, but other aspects of these ideas can be tightened or loosened according to individual family circumstances and the values of its members. But please note: these standards are only effective if they apply to *all* family members, not just the adolescents. Hypocrisy is toxic to strong boundaries and healthy relationships.

1 Alcohol

Alcohol use is not supported until the age of eighteen. And it is *never* acceptable for your teenager to be so intoxicated that they cannot look after themselves no matter what their age (and that goes for parents, too!) as it can be unsafe (think car accidents, poor choices). Adult intoxication is also a problem when children are present as it interferes with parent–child attunement and attachment.

2 Tobacco

Cigarette use is not permissible until the age of eighteen. If cigarettes are found, they will be destroyed. Adolescents aged eighteen and over who choose to smoke (or hang out with smokers) must wash their own clothes or bedding separately. No pocket money will be given to an adolescent who smokes.

3 Sex

There will be no support of sexual intercourse before the age of sixteen. Having a sexual relationship in early adolescence tends to focus the young person on attaching to one person at the expense of developing a wider circle of friends and peer experiences – which is crucial for healthy emotional and social development. Sixteen is also legally the age of consent. Generally (though not universally), sexual intercourse experiences under the age of sixteen tend to be of limited enjoyment as they are often done quickly, furtively, spontaneously and with little playfulness or discussion.

Once adolescents reach sixteen, parents need to decide whether they will allow them to have sexual activity in the family home. In making that decision, it is helpful to consider some historical information on the development of sexual mores. Prior to reliable birth control, sexual activity could result in the creation of a baby. Because of this, most societies have tended to 'castrate their dependents' – anyone who was unable to be independent enough to raise a child was thus not sanctioned by their society to engage in sexual activity. This tended to include children, prisoners, the mentally ill and the intellectually disabled. Birth control and other social changes have made some modifications to this general societal approach, but the deeply ingrained evolved anxiety about a dependent person having sex is unlikely to go away any time soon.

Another thing to consider is that biologically, human beings are sexually mature at around the age of twelve to fourteen. In the distant past this was not a problem as most fourteen-year-olds were independently working with adult responsibilities (the average age of a midshipman in the 1800s was fourteen!) Nowadays, due to education and training, the financial and social independence of young adults can be delayed until as late as the mid-twenties. This mismatch between sexual and social maturity can result in heated disagreements between adolescents and their parents. In handling such disagreement, remember that you don't have to agree with your adolescents, but you do need to listen to them and to try to understand their perspective. (Chapter 9 has more on setting boundaries.)

Also keep in mind that sexual independence is important to young adults, and a strong motivator for them moving out. One family I saw had allowed their young person to sleep with their partner at home, but only under the conditions that the young person would be as discreet as the parents were when they had sex, and would be treated as a fully independent boarder (with 'share-house' rates on rent as well as equal cooking and cleaning responsibilities) – the young person quickly moved out of home. Another family simply bought a caravan for their adolescent to live independently in. Other families have just said 'no', though few were naïve enough to think their young person would not find some way to have sex with their lover. Conversely, many families are okay about their adolescent children having sex in their house for a variety of reasons including safety, and the opportunity to support their young people to see sexuality as something healthy and not to be ashamed of (one mother told me she was 'thrilled' when her daughter said she was sexually active, and even asked her if she enjoyed it!).

In the Netherlands, sexual intercourse is discussed more openly and young women are encouraged to do it when they want to and enjoy it. Empowering young females by talking about sex as enjoyable and desirable may worry some parents. Yet such an approach is associated with the Netherlands having one of the lowest teenage pregnancy rates and lowest sexually transmitted disease rates in the developed world. Also, the average age of first sexual intercourse for a Dutch female is 17.7 in contrast to Australia where it is 16 and in the USA 15.8. Dutch female adolescents were more likely to have intercourse as 'an expression of love', and less likely 'as a way to please others'. And the ability to think about and plan for sex was more strongly related to the use of condoms. In the Netherlands, a parent is often one of the first people a young person tells about their first sexual experience, suggesting it is something to be celebrated rather than something that they are ashamed of or embarrassed about.

I would hypothesise that by being able to talk and think about sex and their desires, they were able to thoughtfully decide what they really wanted using their human brains. In contrast, if sex and desire are repressed due to guilt, shame or fear, then young women are more influenced by their primitive brains, and may make impulsive decisions based on what others want (meeting their need for connection i.e. the mammalian brain), or what they feel like in a given moment (satisfying their sex drive i.e. the reptilian brain).

4 Illicit drugs

Illicit drug use (marijuana, ecstasy, speed etc.) is not acceptable in your house at any age. If illegal drugs are found they will be destroyed. If your child is impaired by substance use then this will be addressed, and no support will be given to peer relationships where drug use plays a part. If family values and rules are unable to contain harmful drug use, then the family will seek out community organisations and ultimately the police to curb the behaviour. Stealing from the family to buy drugs will result in the police being called if reasonable attempts to curb this within the family don't stop it. Keep in mind, though, that experimenting with substances is very common, and for most adolescents doesn't result in significant harm. One third of people will try marijuana in their lifetime and only a small proportion will go on to develop a habit that interferes with their life.

5 Gambling

Gambling is not permissible before the age of eighteen.

6 Pornography

No pornography is to be publicly displayed or publicly available within your house. Pornography is defined as exploitative and unrealistic depictions of sexuality with the intent to cause sexual excitement, and although older teenage boys may privately collect some of these images, they should remain private. There is an obvious disconnect between this standard and our society's values, as many TV ads and billboards display what was once called 'soft porn', and this is unlikely to change as 'sex sells'.

Internet pornography is frequently infantile in the way it views the male and female sexual roles and may have a detrimental effect on your child's developing sexuality and intimate relationships. I suggest that computers are kept in a public place, and strong filter settings used. Witnessing video of other people having sex at a young age and prior to having one's own experiences of sexual relationships is particularly problematic as it sets up unconscious expectations of what sexual experiences 'should' be like (with still images or literature at least some imagination is still required and some naivety remains). So when young people begin to experiment with their partners, the images they have seen (especially if repeated hundreds of times) can have a considerable influence on what they find erotic and enjoyable, and what they expect from, and how they interact with, their sexual partners. The best education about sex is not watching what other people do, but experiencing it for yourself in a relationship characterised by playfulness, acceptance, curiosity and empathy.

CHAPTER 7

PROVIDE ENOUGH UNITY

Unity between the adults in a child's life is crucial, whether it be between two parents, or between parents and other adults such as school staff, paid carers, relatives, coaches, dance teachers and so on.

UNITY BETWEEN PARENTS

The children and adolescents I see with mental health difficulties often have parents or adult carers who are not united as a couple. Disunity can be either the cause of the child's difficulties (as with Tran in the example below), or the result of those difficulties. Either way, without unity between the adults in a family, it is not easy to create an atmosphere in which change can occur.

After meeting safety and basic needs, unity is the most important quality that parents can offer their child.

- Unity is essential when it comes to discipline and helping the child to 'know their place'.
- Unity helps the child give up their intense wish to have a parent all to themselves
- Unity provides a sense of security and predictability to the child.
- Unity models a healthy relationship.

Of course, perfect unity is impossible to attain, and is not desirable, either. Our children benefit greatly from seeing us work together to solve problems and repairing situations that don't go so well. Watching adults compromise is of enormous value to children. It is generally better to be united around an imperfect solution, than to see yourselves as 'right' but in active disunity with the other. We just need to be united enough.

Tran

Nine-year-old Tran lived with his mother and younger brother, and stayed with his father every second weekend. There had been many years of battles with the family court, with claims and counter claims made by both parents about the other parent's inadequacies. His mother brought Tran to see me because she believed he was distressed when he had to see his father, especially at handover times, and this mirrored his mother's distress at letting him go. His mother also found it difficult to control him after visits to his father. The court, through a lengthy process, had decided that the father was a fit parent and insisted that contact occur.

It emerged that Tran liked being with his father, but that the ongoing tension between his parents (who could not even talk to each other) led him to side with his mother when in her presence, and side with his father when in his presence. When alone he stated a wish for them to be back together or at least to 'not fight so much', and that he wanted to see them both.

Rather than engaging in the battle of who was or was not a good parent, I discussed Tran's developmental needs with each parent and their duty to meet those needs and be effective co-parents even if they didn't like each other. Initially I saw the parents separately in preparation for bringing them together to do co-parenting work, and eventually they met together to work out how to be a separated family.

It was tricky for the parents to be in the same room together, and they struggled to keep the focus on their parenting and not attack and criticise each other. But they were able to put their own grievances to one side, put their child first, and managed to develop a co-parenting plan. In the family meetings, they were able to present a united front in which Tran was not put in the impossible position of having to take sides.

The level of distress Tran experienced around transition markedly decreased as he saw his parents cooperate. His oppositional and defiant behaviour initially escalated as he tested his parents' new united resolve, but then gradually subsided as the parents were consistently able, over a number of months, to present a united front.

Unity and discipline

Without unity between the adults in a child's life, values, rules and consequences will have limited effect. And they certainly won't help the child develop the ability to contain themselves and feel secure.

Children look at the adults in their life and feel envy and desire for the power and control the adults seem to have. From an early age we notice in our children their wish to be at least our equals if not our superiors as a way of reversing the power balance.

A fourteen-year-old is not four, but they are also not twenty-four. Though they may wish for adult rights and freedoms, they are not adequately developed to manage the responsibility and stress that goes along with such rights. Adults have the skills to make adult decisions, and children have the skills to make child decisions. If a child finds themselves with the power of an adult, it leaves them in a difficult emotional position. They want the rights and freedoms, but they are ambivalent as the stress and responsibility can be highly anxiety provoking. As an example of this, though you would ask what they wanted you would never give an eight-year-old the right to decide where they should live if their parents have separated. Such a complex decision needs to take into account numerous factors that an eight-year-old cannot adequately understand, let alone decide upon. Instead, the adults in the child's life make this adult decision.

Fourteen-year-olds also have strong wishes and desires without the necessary experience, wisdom and self-control to know how to manage those desires. As an example, the sexual drive at this age is strong, but sexual intimacy with another person at this age would be unhelpful to their development as they lack the necessary maturity to cope with the implications, complications and exclusivity of intimate relationships. A whole bunch of relationship skills need to be learnt and honed in early adolescence (negotiation, compromise, empathy, accepting missing out) if sexual intimacy is to develop in a healthy way. The sexual act is the easy bit, but managing the one-to-one relationship aspect and the emotions it brings up is generally beyond early teenagers, and can result in much pain and suffering.

Our children need to know and be contained within 'their place'. It is the reason why parents intuitively insist that their child use 'please' and 'thank you'. We don't let children take whatever they want; they have to ask permission from the person who has the authority. In childhood that authority is us, but on entering the adult world there are numerous authorities that need to be understood and abided by.

Now, children like being able to do what they want when they want, and they expend a lot of energy trying to get around our authority. They discover through trial and error numerous ways to break the boundaries we put in place to contain their wishes and drives. One of the most effective ways children get around authority is to align themselves with another authority figure who supports their position. 'If Mum won't let me, I'll try Dad.' By obtaining this alignment, it neutralises the other parent's power. The term for this is 'splitting' and it is a very effective technique children use to break down someone's resolve and get what they want.

When children discover the power of parental disunity, it's a technique they will not let go of easily, since the benefits are numerous:

- Once the parents are split, there is a breach in the boundaries and the child can more easily 'get out' of whatever it was the parents were trying to get them to do (or get to do whatever they wanted).
- The parents end up fighting with each other rather than using the energy to contain their child.
- Aligning with one parent against the other can make a child feel particularly close to that parent, thus meeting short-term attachment needs.

- Splitting allows the child to express their anger towards the 'split-off' parent, leaving that parent feeling powerless.
- By being in alignment with a child rather than their partner, the parent effectively gives the child their adult power – not a healthy situation for the child to be in.
- It is easier to argue or fight with a single adult than a united couple ('divide and conquer').

When it comes to parenting a child, all the adults who have a responsibility for the child need to be united. It is one of the reasons that parents (whether separated or not) who are in active conflict often have children who are difficult to manage. If the adults in a child's life don't support each other, the child is able to challenge any adult and their decisions by invoking the name and authority of another adult with comments such as:

- 'Mum says I can go to sleep when I want.'
- 'Dad says I can watch M-rated movies.'
- 'Grandma says I should be going to the other school.'
- 'Grandpa says I shouldn't have to take the tablets if I don't want to.'
- 'My teacher says I should question everything, including what parents say.'
- 'Mum says you are a hopeless teacher who has no idea how to run a classroom.'
- 'The child protection worker says you can't physically stop me from walking out.'
- 'My therapist thinks you are too hard / soft / weak / angry / anxious / etc.'.

Because of all the above, I would suggest you remove the word 'I' from your disciplinary language and replace it with the word 'We'. Not only is it a more powerful word (try it and see), but it also decreases conflict and helps contain the child. 'I' is a person who can be personally attacked. 'We' is a group, and the anger is spread out, diluting the amount of anger directed at any one person.

Unity and healthy relationships

In Chapter 1 we saw that an infant wishes to have their attachment object all to themselves. This desire to be 'the only one' needs to be modified if the child is to develop more mature and healthy relationship patterns. Bit by painful bit they gradually experience loss and disappointment, and give up and grieve their wish to control their attachment object and be the only one.

Of course, we never give up the things we want without a fight because losing what we want is so painful. Between the age of two and five the child's battle to hold onto their special relationship with their attachment object is especially intense, as is their jealousy and wish to cast off anyone they view as competing with their connection to their attachment object such as the other parent, siblings, their parent's friends or their parent's work. Children's play at this time is often filled with aggression. One four-year-old child I saw had a newborn sibling, and during play he would repeatedly put a baby-doll in my office bin. Another would repeatedly try to separate their parents every time they were together in my office. And when a child jumps into bed for a cuddle it is common for them to wriggle into the spot between their parents.

This aggressive wish to 'split' their parents or 'get rid of' their siblings so they get their attachment object to themselves is completely unconscious, yet must be accepted and contained by the adults, as the young child has not yet developed the internal controls to contain themselves. The parents' unity gives the child the clear and firm message, 'You don't get me all to yourself and that's okay.' The child discovers to their relief that the rage they feel when they don't get their parent to themselves does not destroy their parent or result in the other parent attacking them. Instead, they learn that though they don't get everything, they get enough; and enough is okay.

Unity between parents also models that it is okay to argue and disagree. In fact, being in disagreement is quite important as by doing so, we create the opportunity to 'repair' the disconnection. It is during times of repair where dialogue occurs, where differences can be resolved, where understanding is forged, and where creativity in relationships originates. Resolving, repairing and forgiving are vital skills that enable relationships to flourish and grow. Naturally, disagreements without repair have the opposite effect, and are to be avoided as they set up long-term unresolved issues – issues that will likely pop up in future relationships.

Obtaining unity despite disagreement may be difficult at times, but it is one of the most wonderful ways for children to learn how to manage relationships. If our children can learn to resolve conflict, it will aid them in all their relationships, not just within their family but also with friends, employers, lovers etc.

Unity also shows children what a healthy relationship looks like, which makes it less likely they will accept a relationship in the future where they are being dominated, where they are dominating the other person, or where there is chronic disagreement that is not being 'repaired'.

Unity and security

Though disunity benefits the child in their short-term aims of getting their way, in the long term it ends up being an anxiety-provoking experience. Getting mixed messages from parents leaves the child uncertain about what will happen next time an argument occurs, as rarely does one parent always give in to the other. There is no predictability around decision-making and what will happen next. Without this external consistency and predictability, it is harder for the child to develop a sense of internal consistency.

As an example, if one parent lets the child cross the road by themselves and the other parent insists on a parent holding their hand, the child is left wondering what she can and can't do, and can't predict whether she'll get into trouble or not.

Also, when parents are in conflict they sometimes openly involve their children by voicing negative comments about the other parent such as 'She is hopeless' or 'He is such a loser'. However, more often the involvement is covert and subtle. Either way, the children get the message that one parent is unhappy with the other, and will always feel that they have to take sides.

Now, being caught up in other people's conflicts is stressful enough to manage as an adult, and usually leads to a poor outcome for everyone involved, so imagine what it must be like for our children. The many detrimental outcomes for the child include:

- Taking one parent's side and losing the relationship with the other.
- Developing a prominent 'false self' where the child supports each parent in their presence to keep the peace, and feels guilty when in the other parent's presence.
- Being criticised by a parent who believes the child is on the other parent's side.
- Prematurely taking on a 'parental role' in the context of being included in the parental argument. The child may see it as their responsibility to try to resolve the parental conflict and become anxious and even blame themselves for the lack of resolution – which is obviously not good for their self-esteem. It may also set them up in the long term to be a 'rescuer' in other people's relationship conflicts, which compromises their safety and security.

Whatever happens, the child may feel insecure in their relationships, have excessive power over one or both of the parents, and yet ironically may feel completely trapped and unable to effect any change. Whether as children or adults, it is never good to be caught up in someone else's conflicts.

The research supports avoiding involving children in parental conflict, as a significant proportion of the negative outcomes of divorce usually stems from the ongoing acrimony and conflict between separated parents.

If you find yourself in conflict with your child's other attachment objects and the conflict is partly being played out through your child, you have to do whatever it takes to stop this occurring as soon as possible. No amount of counselling will be helpful until this is removed. And if one or both parents refuse to give up the war, the child will suffer for their parents' issues. I have seen adults raging at each other, unable to see that they are doing it over the bodies of their children.

UNITY WITH OTHER ADULTS

Unity is also necessary between all the adults who have responsibility for the child, including relatives, paid carers, teachers, coaches, clinicians and any healthcare or legal workers involved. Most of the points already covered are relevant to these relationships, but a few specific suggestions follow.

School staff

School is one of the most important developmental experiences our children have. They spend thousands of hours there, and are strongly influenced by an array of adults and peers. It influences their development cognitively, emotionally, relationally and physically, providing a vital setting in which they develop their sense of 'self'.

School may, of course, be a difficult place for some children and at times they may refuse to attend. Acute and persistent school refusal is considered to be a 'psychiatric emergency' by mental health services, and a united approach is essential to resolve it. Without that unity, the chance of getting the child back to school is significantly decreased.

Teachers are delegated many parental rights and responsibilities for the children in their care, which parents implicitly agree to when they send their child to school. However, if parents do not support the staff, the school is weakened in its ability to put in place adequate boundaries, enabling some children to get away with inappropriate behaviour that a united approach would help to contain. Often the most behaviourally disturbed children are those whose parents have no contact with the school, despite frequent attempts by staff. When I speak to the parents of these children they are often scathingly critical of the school; the reverse is the case when I speak to the school. It is not good enough to complain and blame the other, and simply wait for the other to change.

If there is a lack of unity, the parents and the school must do whatever it takes to obtain it, or the child will suffer ongoing problems. Getting a united understanding and approach to a particular child may be as simple as a corridor chat, or as complex as a case conference involving parents, teachers, psychiatrists and the department of education.

I would strongly recommend that both parents attend school meetings, parent–teacher interviews and any disciplinary meetings, whether they are separated or not. By doing so, they can be clear in their minds that the school has a united approach with their own; it shows the school that the parents are serious about supporting it in its work and it puts appropriate pressure on all parties to find a way ahead together. And finally, it gives the child the clear message that when it comes to school, the adults in his life are united and support each other.

In the end, after all attempts have been made, if the school or the parents are unable to achieve unity then the parents have the responsibility to find another setting in which unity is achievable. This of course will have a destabilising effect on the child, so it should be avoided if possible.

The child's wishes are to be listened to, taken into account and supported as much as is reasonable, but in the end while a child is dependent on the adults in their life, the decision of schooling must be the adults', not the child's.

Relatives

Relatives, especially grandparents, are important for our children. They are a source of wisdom, support, love and kindness, and in difficult times they can come through when friends are not always able to help. As the saying goes, blood is thicker than water, though I would add that at times it is also messier!

Parents often complain to me that close family members don't support their parenting strategies, and this can become an issue if a child is regularly cared for by those family members. However, as the parent, it is your responsibility to set up the environment you want for your child. And if you see a family member going against what you want in a way that matters (don't sweat the small stuff; celebrate difference unless it is undermining), it is your responsibility to do whatever it takes to correct that.

The more time you leave your child in your relative's care, the more important a united approach is, and the same principles apply as for our interaction with teachers. In such a discussion, keep the focus on the importance of a united approach and your wish to work with the other person to obtain that.

This is not always easy to do, but usually the affection you have for each other and the shared affection for your child helps resolve the issue. If you are unable to obtain a united approach, you have to ask yourself whether you feel comfortable leaving your child in the care of someone you don't and can't agree with.

Paid carers

As our lives get busier, sometimes we pay other people to care for and help our child, e.g. childcare workers, nannies, babysitters, therapists, tutors, coaches etc. Just as with school, we need to be convinced that the adults our children are being left with are appropriate role models who share our values. Generally it is fairly safe to assume that other adults are going to be appropriate, but if you have any concerns about this, the answer is not to complain, but to do whatever it takes to obtain the unity your children require, otherwise, you withdraw your child from their care. There is no other reasonable alternative to this. I am aware that this takes time, may be difficult, uncomfortable and even tedious. And your child may miss out if a united approach can't be agreed upon, leading to tense times with them. But the upfront cost pays for itself when a united approach is needed.

A values mismatch?

One family I saw had their six-year-old enrolled in a dance class, and they were going to sing and perform a tap routine to an old song 'All the nice girls love a sailor'.

The father thought the title sounded a bit odd, but went with the flow – until he saw the lyrics. At the very bottom he read, 'And you *can* trust a sailor, he's a white man all the while!'

What to do? His six-year-old loved the class, but could he let her sing this clearly racist song?

He telephoned the teacher to express his concern, and added that if the song or words weren't changed, he couldn't in all conscience allow his daughter to be part of the performance. (He'd resigned himself to dealing with his daughter's distress when it came.)

Fortunately, there was a happy ending. The teacher hadn't actually read through to the end of the lyrics, and was horrified by them, too, and the song was changed.

At first their values seemed to be at odds, but a quick chat revealed enough unity for his daughter to continue in the class.

HANDLING DISUNITY

If there is disunity between you and your partner, or you and another adult in your child's life, there are things you can do to help achieve greater unity.

- Know yourself: your strengths and weaknesses; your expectations and values. 'What do I want?' The stronger and more certain you are about what you want, the more you will be able to enter any disunity with respectful firmness, rather than emotional defensiveness. Get your own support if you need it.
- Live for yourself, and don't expect others to live for you. You need to have an approach and self-belief that doesn't rely on others' permission or reassurance.
- Don't be a mind-reader and don't expect others to read your mind. You will need to be explicit about what you think and what you want.
- Clarify the issue towards which you and the other adult need to be united. Write it down if necessary as this can help.
- Approach the discussion with your human brain fully turned on. If your reptilian brain (fear) or mammalian brain (insecurity) is too active, it will be hard to think. If during the discussion your feelings overwhelm you, stop the discussion (unity will be impossible if one of you cannot think) and take a break: 'I want to talk about this, but I'm not calm enough right now.'
- Initially try an informal approach and assume that the other

person will also want to sort it out for the children's sake (this is not always the case, but is worth trying). Discuss the issue when the children are not going to interrupt and when both adults are not busy, stressed or preoccupied.

- If unity is not achieved the first time, make another time when the issue can be discussed again.
- Remember to cut the other adult some slack: you may have been thinking about this issue for weeks or months, while they may have had only a day or so (or less) and are feeling a bit defensive. It is generally useful to have some time between discussing the problem for the first time and coming to a resolution.
- Keep reminding yourself and the other adult that you are only bringing this up for the children's' sake. Focusing on what the children need can help keep personal issues between the adults out of the argument – at least a bit.
- If the simple chat doesn't work or emotions are too high, increase the formality and keep increasing it until unity is achieved. If an informal discussion doesn't work, have a planned meeting, then a planned meeting with a mediator, and keep going up the formality chain, if necessary getting to the family court if the issue around which you disagree is important enough.
- If an adult says, 'I just don't want to talk about it', think about whether this is reasonable or not. Avoiding the disunity won't make it go away – it just delays the after-effects. Allowing avoidance confirms to the other adult that it is really your problem, and if they push enough you will back down and fix it yourself. Effectively you are saving the other adult from the problem. Nice of you, but not nice for you.

I have seen lots of parents who, because of their love for their child and not wishing for them to suffer, fill the gap left by another adult's incompetence and everyone suffers from the disunity this usually brings. I have heard about parents making excuses for the other parent for missed birthdays and events, buying presents saying they were from the other person, even forging Christmas cards.

You provide a poor model for your child if you allow another adult to dump their responsibility on you. If you think there is a gap between what the other adult should be doing and is doing, your job is not to fill that gap but to bring the gap to the other adult's attention and gently but firmly leave that problem with them. If the gap continues, then your job is to support your child as they suffer from missing out on the things they need from the other adult. Don't criticise the other adult, but don't defend them either.

Ultimately, where two adults with equal rights and responsibilities for a child cannot agree on an important point despite all efforts, a third party with authority needs to be engaged to make the decision. Some extended families and cultural groups have an authority figure who can take this role. If this is not available or not appropriate, the involvement of more formal dispute resolution agencies may be required such as the family court.

CHAPTER 8

PROVIDE ENOUGH AFFECTIONATE CARE

After the need to feel safe, have basic needs met, and to experience unity among carers, the next most important provision for your child's development is affection and care. It may sound obvious, but children need their parents/carers to spend time with them, share experiences with them and to show them kindness and affection. You don't have to entertain them (that's their job), but you do have to be interested in them.

There are many reasons why affection is crucial for children:

- It helps builds their self-esteem and confidence when given generously and without conditions: 'I am valuable for who I am, not just what I do.'
- It helps them feel attached to you, allowing them to use more positive and subtle attachment behaviours, especially playfulness and humour, rather than more negative and obvious ones, such as provocation or control. (See 'Attachment Behaviours' in Chapter 1 for more information.)
- It provides an important balance for when you need to discipline them. There is a place where people regularly experience discipline without care; it's called jail – a place most people want to get out of, and where relationships between the authorities

> and inmates is usually quite tense. Boundaries put in place by someone who cares about you are much easier to accept than those put in place by someone who appears to think poorly of you. I always address a child's care needs before their containment needs, as generally it is best if we care before we correct.

Your child's belief that you think well of them and expect good things from them is a powerful yet underestimated motivator of their behaviour. As little children their sense of being okay is strongly tied to your approval of what they do. You are their mirror, and how they perceive themselves is related to how you see them. They are built up by your praise, and devastated by your criticism. As they grow, they start to think for themselves, to do things that are recognised by others, and to develop self-approval, but that primitive wish for your approval remains in their unconscious so that even as an adult, a parent saying 'Well done' can be a deeply satisfying emotional experience.

As they mature, they become more ambivalent about what you think (and will probably tell you how little they care about your opinion). But we know better than to take such statements at face value. The wish to not care what you think is part of their developing individuation; an attempt to balance the fact that they care so much.

So let me spell it out again: deep down your child will always care what you think about them, and will always wish to have your approval. Don't be fooled by your child's rejection and denials – of course they care what you think, and all the more so if you show them that you think they are great.

Love is not enough if you don't show it, or your child does not experience it. You need to let them know that you think they are great and that you are proud of them. If they do make mistakes that need correcting, it should be done in a way that is balanced with their experience that you care about them and believe that things can be different. This is often quite difficult. We often say, 'I'm angry at the behaviour, not the person', but that is your human brain talking. When we are angry and our emotions are high, our mammalian and reptilian brains are not able to distinguish between the action and the person, and the spilling of milk over the table can so easily lead to the angry reactive criticism of, 'You are so clumsy' versus a more thoughtful reflection of, 'That was a clumsy move, honey.' That is why, as much as possible, we need to react less and reflect more (see Chapter 10).

Frances

Ten-year-old Frances had always been a handful. She was a smart and active young girl, but struggled with her emotions and was easily disappointed, which often led to her having tantrums that included throwing things and hitting. A year before I saw her, she had thrown a cup of boiling water on her younger brother while they were alone together in the kitchen, causing burns to his face that required multiple medical appointments and resulted in some scarring.

After the burning, Frances was remorseful and initially her behaviour improved. However, as the year progressed, she became increasingly moody and her behaviour worsened. Her parents' old disciplinary strategies were failing, and they were at a loss to know how to manage her outbursts. In desperation, they took to shutting her out in the backyard to 'protect her brother'.

When I saw Frances on her own, she said she didn't believe her parents loved her anymore. They no longer did nightly book reading with her, and she claimed her father never talked to her. She said she was sometimes naughty to 'get them back'.

When I spoke to her parents, they confirmed that they still felt furious with Frances and found it difficult to even look at her at times. Although they'd told Frances that they forgave her, both admitted to ongoing anger and resentment. They identified a link between attending the brother's medical appointments, their increased anger, and Frances's subsequently worsening behaviour.

A family therapy approach was employed in which the scalding and subsequent events were discussed openly, along with each person's feelings about them. It turned out the burnt brother was the least angry and distressed.

> Over the next few sessions the parents were able to model forgiveness and repair the relationships through tears and laughter. Over time Frances felt a valued part of the family again and discipline gradually became easier.

THE BASICS OF CARING ENOUGH

In some homes, the issue is not that parents do not love or care for the child, but that they don't *show* their affection enough and the child therefore does not experience it enough. There can be a parental style of avoiding emotional intimacy and focusing on discipline that goes back generations. If as a child you believed you were not thought well of, it may make it more difficult for you to openly praise and show affection to your own children.

In these settings, the amount of emotion that goes into disciplining the child can be quite high, whereas the amount of emotion that goes into encouraging them is comparatively low. If, for example, a child who has behaved well hears 'good job' and feels a two-second ruffle of his hair, but when he behaves badly gets a fifteen-minute lecture angrily pointing out all his faults, it is obvious which emotional experience is likely to have a greater influence on how he feels about himself.

The aim is to increase the frequency and emotional intensity of praise and affection, and to diminish the frequency and emotional intensity of discipline and correction. However, this is not to say that a child should be praised and shown affection willy-nilly. Excessive praise and care can be a problem, too. Remember, the aim is to care *enough*. Some parents mollycoddle their child to save them from missing out and having to suffer. As we have seen in earlier chapters, this interferes with their healthy development, since the child rarely gets to take initiative, cope with successes and failures, and learn how to get over disappointment and their absurd wish to be special.

Share experiences and stories

It is often suggested that we spend 'quality time' with our children, focusing intently on them and our relationship with them, but this is usually for relatively brief periods. Children also need 'quantity time' – to simply be with us, whatever we are doing.

Sharing experiences and stories with our children not only supports their attachment to us, but also creates memories. For children, the memory of these experiences forms a part of the 'story' of themselves and their relationships – an important part of their developing identity.

Think about your own experiences with people important to you: the holidays you have shared, the spontaneous meals you've had together, sporting or artistic triumphs you have witnessed, bands you have seen, weddings or other milestone celebrations you've attended. These shared experiences, along with telling people about these experiences, are like a kind of glue, keeping you connected with others even when the years intervene. In effect, when another person shares your experience, they validate it: 'I was there. Your story happened.' The glue of shared experiences helps give a sense of togetherness, 'We did it together. You are not alone.' If you are at their triumphs and tragedies, you can witness, confirm, explain and support them not only at the time, but also into the future.

As children grow up, increasingly we will not be part of their experiences and this is appropriate as their life extends beyond their family. But they still need us to be interested and to bear witness to their struggles and successes (even if it is by phone or email, rather than being there in person), and to help them share and make sense of their story. So it is important that you turn up to their events, eat together, go on holidays, celebrate successes and simply talk together and share stories. Don't be so busy that you don't get to share enough experiences with your child. Four hours sitting through a gymnastics display (let me tell you) is dull, dull, dull; but being there when your child gets their participation medal is gold for you and your child.

Give them one-on-one time

Your children have to come to terms with the awful truth that they are not special and not the only one, but that does not mean they don't need one-on-one time with you. On the contrary, it is quite important that each child gets time alone with each parent on a regular basis.

As is frequently mentioned throughout this book, it is about finding the balance and them getting enough.

Though it can be uncomfortable to admit, some children are easier than others to spend time with and to give affection to. It can be especially challenging if you have a child who tends to blame you as a way of dealing with their own unmet expectations or who complains about not spending time with you or things not being fair, but when you do spend time with them or give in to their demands, they criticise or reject you. And their rejection of our care can easily result in us rejecting them back in return: 'Why do you have to spoil everything?' Even the most aware parent cannot help taking such behaviour personally at times. It is easy to see how a vicious cycle develops in such situations: the child predicts rejection, which leads to actual rejection, reinforcing the child's belief that they are rejected, and the expectation that they will always be rejected, and so on it goes.

So if your child's behaviour often makes it difficult to be with them, you need to prepare yourself and to keep providing positive one-on-one interactions even when you don't feel like it. This is easier said than done, but I cannot overstate how critical it is for your child to feel likeable and securely connected to you.

It is far better to have a regular, short time together that is positive, than to have an irregular, large slab of time that is inconsistent. A weekly weekend café visit that almost always happens and can be predictably looked forward to is more connecting than spontaneous café visits that can happen two or three times a week but then not for a month or two.

Here are a few more tips regarding one-on-one time:

- Walking together can be connecting, but start with a ten-minute walk to the local shops and back rather than a two-hour hike.
- Cooking something together is great, but start with ten-minute biscuits, not an intricate and difficult dinner.
- Playing a game is also good one-on-one time, but choose a fifteen-minute game like Uno, Go Fish or Snakes and Ladders – not games like Monopoly (which can take hours).

- Try to make your one-on-one time similar for each child. Whatever you give one child is likely to be wanted by their siblings, but it will be impossible for it to be perfectly fair (an absurd wish that is only desired by those who perceive they get less, never by those who get more).
- It is vital that your children experience you having one-to-one time with your partner to reinforce the idea that everyone gets special one-on-one time, and everyone misses out. I generally advise a monthly 'date night'; whether it helps the kids or not, it's good for you and your partner.

Be on their side

Your children will make mistakes, they will be messy, they will say and do the wrong thing, they will make bad decisions, they will hit a playmate, they will be selfish, they will lie, they won't wait their turn – in short, they will do things that are at times annoying, embarrassing and shaming to both themselves and you. As parents we often excessively identify with our children and judge ourselves and are judged by others according to our children's behaviour. Even when our adult children get into trouble it is not uncommon to hear us say, 'Where did I go wrong?'

In situations where your child has an accident or makes a mistake it is important that your first response is to back up your child – to show you are on her side. Because of your own feelings you may want to point out her faults immediately, but try to avoid doing this. Your child will probably be hyper-aware of her mistake or accident and feel ashamed (even if she is covering it up by acting as if she doesn't care). If it was an accident, then your support will be welcome. If she was at fault, your initial support will be helpful for the later discussion about what went wrong, even if a consequence needs to be put in place (see 'Externalising the Rules' on page 156 for more about setting consequences). Your child may or may not benefit from any advice you have to offer, but she will *always* benefit from knowing that no matter what happens, you will be on her side.

Your children need you to trust them and to take their side. If *you* don't back them up who will? And if you don't back them up they may develop the unfortunate belief that they are not worthy of being supported. If you do not trust them enough, they may develop a view that they cannot trust themselves, or that others cannot be trusted. If in doubt, err on the side of backing up and trusting too much rather than too little.

Adrian

One young adult I worked with suffered from extreme self-doubt, anxiety and self-loathing. Adrian told me that he'd been relentlessly bullied at school, but that whenever he'd told his mother about it, her first response had always been, 'But what were you doing that made them bully you?' If he made a decision that involved another person, she would always ask him how that decision would make the other person feel. Adrian's mother seemed to always find fault in him and took the other person's side, not only telling him how he was in the wrong, but also what he should do to remedy the situation. In one session, while quite distressed, he said, 'I didn't need her to tell me what was right and wrong or what to do; I just wanted her to be on my side.' Together we worked on Adrian trying to change and repair what could be changed and repaired in his adult relationship with his mother (unfortunately not that much); to grieve and accept what couldn't be changed; and ultimately for Adrian to parent himself and be on his own side.

Care first, then correct

If your child has actually behaved inappropriately, the general approach would be to protect, care and comfort him first (in other words, deal with his reptilian and mammalian brains) and then to correct his behaviour using clear reasoning and consequences (i.e. his human brain). As mentioned earlier, it is an easier experience to be 'corrected' by someone who you feel cares for you. It is for this reason that we need to balance enough care with enough correction:

strong correction goes best with strong affection; strong correction with low affection is like jail.

Of course, the tendency to react and correct first will be strong, especially if the child has done something provocative and infuriating. If you do find yourself in the middle of a knee-jerk angry response (for example, after they run into the car with their bike and do a few hundred dollars worth of damage), don't beat yourself up too much – it's totally understandable to react. However, as soon as you can, take a deep breath, apologise for yelling or swearing (or however your anger manifests) and let them know that whatever happened can be sorted out. Once emotions are calmed and you are both thinking again, then you can address the problem: 'You are in huge trouble for scratching the car and we have to think about what to do about it.' Caring for them first does not mean the problem gets blown over and forgotten, it just means that when the correction occurs it is done in a thoughtful rather than an emotional way.

Children who are corrected without care (such as from a stern parent, teacher, coach or boss) tend to feel either shameful anger towards themselves, or defensive anger towards the correcting person. Either way, the anger prevents their ability to reflect on and think about the situation in a healthy way. However, caring *before* correcting teaches children that even if we are disciplining them, we still back them up, trust them and believe that they can get over this mistake and learn from it. It also makes the correction more likely to have a positive learning effect, so less likely to happen again.

Forgive them

If your children too easily disappoint you, change your approach:

- Be more playful and less serious about their mistakes.
- Be more accepting of where they are at – high expectations makes it more likely that they won't measure up.
- Be more curious about what happened and less certain that your point of view is always 'right'.
- Be aware of their feelings, and approach them with empathy.

Forgiveness is the opposite of holding a grudge caused by disappointment. The resentment and impulse to punish those who have hurt us is powerful, and forgiveness is the letting go of this need or desire to seek revenge. The gift of forgiveness is beyond measure as it allows the repair of important relationships, it supports the development of intimacy with others (nothing is more toxic to a relationship than holding a grudge), and most importantly, shows your child *how* to forgive. Through repairing, your child learns that difficulties and disappointments can be 'gotten over', shame becomes less powerful, and self-esteem is enhanced.

However, if a child or adolescent has behaved in such a cruel, aggressive or hurtful way that we see them in a negative light, it is up to *us* to take the lead in repairing the damage and finding a way of viewing them more positively. We are the adults in these situations and we are responsible for looking after the needs of the young person in our care.

Thus, when your child hurts you, try to see it as an opportunity to model how to forgive and repair. As we saw in Chapter 4, making mistakes – 'messing up' – is a cause for celebration for all of us (not only our children), as we learn most during the process of repair.

WHAT IF THE CHILD IS NOT THOUGHT WELL OF?

Sometimes a parent or guardian does not think well enough of their child, and there can be many reasons for this.

- The parent may have not experienced positive regard from their own parent and find it difficult to give to their child what they didn't receive themselves.
- The parent may have a mental illness or substance-abuse problem. In such cases the parent is often so preoccupied with their own issues that they barely register their child's existence, let alone acknowledge them in a positive way. People with numbness from post-traumatic stress disorder often struggle to have any feelings, let alone loving feelings. Depression tends to consume the sufferer's mind, making it hard to think about anyone

but themselves. Anxiety is a mind killer, and frequently steals joy and playfulness. Intoxication numbs the mind, and leads to a decrease in the awareness of others and what their needs might be. In all these situations, there is the tendency for the child to be forgotten or overlooked, and the subtle interplay between the child and the parent ceases to be effective. Trying to get on a depressed, anxious or intoxicated parent's mind to feel secure and safe requires some heavy-duty attachment behaviours, and these may not always be positive ones (see '"The Cry" Attachment Behaviours' on page 15).

- Some parents have personality disorders that make it hard to experience positive feelings towards others. The narcissistic parent struggles to see the child as anything beyond a tool for their own uses. In such situations, the child learns that the only way to get his needs for closeness met is by being the 'thing' (false self) that his parent wishes him to be, and any attempt to assert his own desires (true self) is met with a loss of closeness or with active rejection. The parent with borderline personality disorder tends to view their child as 'all good' or 'all bad', and switches their responses from positive to negative without warning. This can result in the child feeling deeply insecure and uncertain about their worth.
- For other parents, certain disabilities and disorders in their child also make having positive feelings more difficult, such as an intellectual disability, the pervasive developmental disorders such as autism and Asperger's syndrome, physically deforming disorders, or acquired brain injury. Parental guilt about having these mixed feelings complicates how their child is viewed, too.
- Some parents unconsciously identify their children with people they have loathed or feared such as ex-partners, other family members, friends, or parts of themselves that they do not like. I have heard a three-year-old being described as 'just like his father' (her partner was physically abusive). In cases like these, the 'bad' aspects of a person are projected onto the child, leaving the parent feeling negatively towards the child. A mother once

> told me her two-month-old baby was trying to 'dominate her'. This said more about the mother's mind-set than the infant's behaviour.

Don't get me wrong. It's okay to have negative feelings about your child's *behaviour* when it disappoints or provokes you. Like the pain you experience when you touch a hot stove, these feelings are not right or wrong; they are simply telling you something. Our adult task is to understand, tolerate, reflect on, and get over these feelings, and then move on to helping the child modify their behaviour (see the next chapter).

If you struggle to have positive feelings towards your children as human beings, then you need to do whatever it takes to develop those feelings or to remove the things that are blocking out those feelings. If it only happens occasionally, there are many informal ways to overcome negative feelings and develop more positive ones.

- Share one-on-one time with them (children love to have your attention and just chatting to them can bring out the best in both of you).
- Talk to a supportive friend about how you feel.
- Take a playful and repairing approach to life in general; increasing playfulness and forgiveness encourages positive feelings towards those we interact with.
- Approach interactions with respect and dignity; treating others with respect and dignity encourages positive feelings in both giver and receiver.

However, if negative feelings towards a child are persistent and all-pervasive, professional help is necessary. This may involve psychotherapy or counselling for specific difficulties or illnesses, or parent therapy to explore what it is about being a parent that makes it difficult for you to provide enough positive affection.

CHAPTER 9

PROVIDE ENOUGH BOUNDARIES

There is an old saying, 'Take what you want and pay for it.' This is a vital learning experience for our children: they *can* do whatever they want as long as they are willing to pay the price. They can hit their brother, draw on the walls, smash the glass, or sneak out of the house at night, but only if they are willing to suffer the consequences.

As we saw in Part 1, young children tend to believe that their parents will clean up all their messes and fix all their mistakes, and this is generally true for the very young. But as children grow, they must learn that *they* are accountable for their own actions. As parents, we gradually move from a position of saving (preventing a mess or cleaning it up when it happens) to supporting them (letting them make their own mess and supporting them to clean it up themselves). This slow shift from saving to supporting is difficult both for our children and for us. Watching our child make bad decisions is one of the more difficult tasks of parenting.

One way to help our children and ourselves manage this transition is by having clear and predictable boundaries that we all stick to.

Little children have few internal boundaries and minimal self-control. They want what they want when they want it with little regard for whether it is helpful and reasonable or not. Their ability to manage their more intense emotions and uncontrolled behaviours when they miss out or are disappointed is still very weak. We step in and save them from themselves by providing rules to guide them in what is and is not allowed. If when they are small they experience these boundaries as predictable, consistent and helpful, they gradually take them on and begin to control themselves rather than needing the control of others. Instead of us telling them what to do, they begin to tell themselves what to do.

There are many strategies to contain our children when they are overwhelmed with their emotions of insecurity, loss and disappointment, and their behaviour is unreasonable. Whatever strategies you choose to use in your family, you must be united with your partner and committed to implementing them, and they must, over time, help your child learn to control themselves rather than needing to be enforced by others.

Punishments such as smacking or threatening to leave children behind if they don't hurry up usually stop unwanted behaviour in the short term (at least the first few times), but do little to help children control their own behaviour except through fear of further hitting or abandonment. And as previously learnt, a fear response works in a more primitive part of the brain where thinking and planning have little effect. These boundaries simply reinforce in a child's mind 'What does my parent want?' to which they will react by either fearfully obeying, or angrily resisting.

As an alternative to fearful punishments, logical consequences such as not replacing a mistreated broken toy or withholding pocket money for neglected chores may not resolve unwanted behaviour immediately, but they help set up a situation where children may reflect on their own actions and the outcomes that occurred. The next time they are playing with a toy they may be more careful; or when it is time to do their chores they may do them whether a parent is present or not. They are motivated by their own thoughts and experiences about their options rather than by the thoughts and feelings of their parent. Instead of thinking, 'What does my parent want?' they are more likely to be thinking, 'What do I think is best for me?'

The ultimate aim of setting boundaries is that we do ourselves out of a job. 'Growing up' is thus the gradual process of moving from needing to be parented by others into becoming one's own parent.

Broadly speaking, there are two steps to setting boundaries:

1 to externalise the rules, so that boundaries are essentially agreed rules that are not made up on the go; and
2 to base the rules on values, so that boundaries are based on what *is* wanted (the value) rather than what is *not* wanted (the rule).

These approaches are not only effective, but also help children to regulate themselves rather than needing regulation by others – the ultimate aim of any discipline strategy.

Adam

Nine-year-old Adam lived with his parents. They described him as a 'terror' who ran the house, and when they saw me they seemed exhausted and quite defeated. 'We've tried everything, and nothing works. Would medication help?'

I assessed Adam and he didn't have a mental illness that would benefit from medication. Indeed, at school and at other people's houses he was described as a model child. Rather, he came across as a deeply insecure boy who coped with his feelings by using bravado and controlling behaviour.

During the assessment phase he tried to control the interview on numerous occasions, and when I contained him with simple boundaries, his anxiety and anger at not getting his way rapidly escalated until he left the room and told his parents, 'We're not coming back.' Fortunately, by the time he left the assessment was complete, and it was clear that initially, the work would be with his parents.

The first step was to encourage Adam's parents to see their son differently – to 'reframe' him as an insecure little boy who used control as a way of keeping his anxiety at bay, rather than a terrible boy who controlled through malice. They took some convincing!

Although they cared deeply for their boy, and their family was a safe place, with enough ritual and unity, it soon became clear that both parents were brought up in cold and controlling families, and both remembered thinking to themselves in adolescence, 'When I'm a parent I will *never* be like my parents!' The parents took on an exceptionally permissive parenting style, relying on reason to guide Adam's behaviour. Now this could have worked for many children, but Adam's active temperament and precocious intelligence meant he had learned from an early age how to get around his parents' attempts to contain him. He was also very inquisitive and stubborn.

Adam's parents were furious, but his father (who it emerged was quite scared he might become violent like his own father) withdrew to his room when he became angry, increasing Adam's already powerful position, while at the same time increasing his insecurity and reinforcing his controlling attachment behaviours.

Much work was done with the parents, and over time they gradually increased Adam's containment with clear boundaries (with a few hiccups along the way). Six months later Adam was less powerful and more contained, the parents were more relaxed, and Adam was obviously less anxious and better behaved at home.

EXTERNALISING THE RULES

In most families, the rules and consequences that apply to the children are determined by what the parents say. For example:

Rule: 'I've told you not to hit your sister.'

Consequence: 'I'm banning you from the computer/DS/Xbox for twenty-four hours.'

The child experiences the rules and consequences as being generated by the parent – 'your rules'. This means that when the child 'breaks' the rules, they are in effect 'breaking' the parent, who often experiences the disobedience as a direct attack on them. This can partly explain why we become so angry when our children disobey us ('I told you not to do it!').

Similarly, when the parent enforces the consequences, the child experiences this as an attack by the parent, which explains partly why children get so angry. Both parent and child feel attacked, typically resulting in an emotional reaction, which often triggers further transgressions, resulting in greater need to enforce rules and consequences, and so the cycle continues.

The alternative to rules coming from inside the parent (internalised) is to externalise them. This is where the rules and consequences are decided by the whole family, and are written on a piece of paper. In this way the rules are no longer 'my' rules but become 'our rules', 'family rules' or 'the rules we decided on'. The same goes for the consequences of breaking those rules.

So when a family member (including a parent) breaks the rules, they are not attacking the parent but a piece of paper or a crystal clear agreement. And when the consequences are enforced, they are being 'attacked' by that same piece of paper or agreement. The legal system works in the same way: the judge controls the courtroom and ensures that the law is followed, but it is not the judge's law that is broken or the judge's consequences that are implemented, but those of 'the law' – the collection of our society's rules over many years that we as a community have decided on (through our political system). Because of this, the judge can be impartial and even supportive of the defendant despite, say, sending them to jail; and the defendant knows they are being punished by 'the law', and not by the judge. Rarely is a judge abused, attacked or provoked, despite them enforcing some devastating consequences. And the judge does not feel personally affronted by the defendant's behaviour, as the defendant is disobeying the law, not the judge's personal rules.

In the same way, behavioural guidelines in your home become '*the* rules' rather than '*my* rules'. And when implementing the consequences, you can remain on your child's side. Here are some examples showing the difference between rules that are internalised ('my rules') and externalised ('our rules'):

My rules: 'I told you to finish your homework! That's it: no Internet for you tonight!'

Our rules: 'I wanted you to have time on the Internet tonight as I know you enjoy it. But you didn't finish your homework and the rules on the fridge are clear that if you don't, there is no Internet.'

My rules: 'How many times do I have to tell you not to swear at me? I'm taking $2 from your pocket money this week!'

Our rules: 'The rules say to deduct $2 from your pocket money for swearing. A shame really, as I know you are saving for that Nintendo game. I hope next week you won't break the rules and you'll get the $2.'

In both examples the young person may get angry, but where the rules are clear and external to the parent, the young person can only really be angry at themselves.

The advantages of externalised rules

- You stay connected to your child and on their side, despite containing them.
- You feel less attacked, so your reptilian brain will be quieter and you will be able to thoughtfully reflect, rather than emotionally react. This means you are less likely to become angry yourself, which in turn means there is less likelihood of conflict escalating to feed the negative cycle of conflict (i.e. leading to more breaking of boundaries, leading to more conflict and so on).
- You are also less likely to say things that will give your children the message that they are a disappointment and lead to them feeling ashamed or defensively enraged and reacting emotionally. They are more likely to be reflecting on the situation.
- You are more able to stay calm yet firm as you aren't caught on the hop having to make up on-the-spot rules and consequences.
- The rules and consequences will be more predictable and appropriate because they are written down or clearly stated after thoughtful discussion, rather than being made in a flash of anger or frustration. ('Grounding for life' may feel like the right response at the time, but probably isn't the best idea!)
- Your children are more likely to think twice before doing the wrong thing as they begin to know with certainty what will happen if they take a certain course of action – aiding the development of self-control and self-restraint.

- Your children have clear boundaries to push against, which is important in teaching them where the boundaries are. In this sense, we can celebrate when boundaries are tested and broken as it allows an opportunity to talk about the boundary and negotiate a compromise, or to not compromise and allow our children to be disappointed and have to accept and get over it.
- Your children are less likely to reject the rules and consequences ('But they are your rules on the paper!') because they have been created together by the whole family.
- Your children gradually learn to choose certain actions not to please others or avoid disappointment, but because they have decided it is what they think they should do. This is one of your long-term goals as a parent: to help your children grow up and become their own parents.

The warring sisters

A family whose two young girls kept hitting each other came to see me. 'Nothing works to stop them,' I was told. We went through each of the disciplinary strategies they had tried, and all of them seemed reasonable (if a little inconsistent and excessive), and all had worked for a day or two, but then stopped working.

I looked at their overall approach (see Chapter 4), and though the family had a sense of humour and showed a lot of care and empathy, the mother in particular could not accept that her daughters would want to hit each other. 'They even do it in public; it is so embarrassing.' Her expectations of good behaviour were high ('My mother would never have allowed us to do it'), and she found herself particularly enraged when the older sister targeted the younger one.

It came as no surprise to learn that she had an older sister who had put her down, but only when their mother was not around. When angry at her own children she punished them with whatever came to mind, and the angrier she was the harsher the consequence, especially towards the older girl.

A lot of the parenting work we did was to help the mother to understand her children's and her own emotional responses, and adding 'accepting rather than expecting' into her repertoire of approaches. Then we put the strategy in place.

It was actually quite simple. Both parents met with the girls and explained that the hitting had to stop. They told the children that they accepted that the girls at times disliked each other and felt like hitting, but that they could not hit each other anymore. 'We don't hit people in this family.' If they chose to hit each other, there would be a twenty-four-hour TV ban from the moment of hitting for them both, no matter who did it or why the hitting occurred. Favourite shows could be taped to watch later. If the hitting did not stop after one week, a new, stronger consequence would be devised for the next week and the week after that.

The parents asked the children if this needed to be written down, but the children felt it was just too easy to remember: 'If either of us hit, both of us lose TV for twenty-four hours.' The rule and consequence was now crystal clear, and no longer created at the mother's whim, but was the whole family's idea.

The first week was pretty rough: there was no TV for five straight days. Then they got TV for two days, then lost it for two days, then got it back for six days. It took two months, but the hitting eventually became a very rare occurrence.

On asking the mother why she thought the change had occurred, she replied, 'It was no longer my problem, but their problem. I didn't give them permission to hit each other, but I accepted that they were. I stopped expecting them not to, so I became less frustrated. Yet I still had control over the consequences, and knew what to do when the hitting happened. The only ones getting hurt by their actions were themselves, and they decided for themselves it just wasn't worth it.'

CREATING VALUES-BASED BOUNDARIES

So, how do you create helpful external rules and consequences? You do it by first being clear about what you want (the value) and how this directly leads on to what you don't want (the rule); and then working out whatever it is going to take to stop the value from being broken (the consequence). This is best done together as a family (unless the children are preschoolers) rather than being imposed on children without them having any say.

Establishing boundaries is usually straightforward, but simple mistakes can render them ineffectual, and children are usually quite skilled at finding weak points. Parents sometimes say to me, 'But I've tried these things and they don't work!' In my experience, when someone says boundaries do not work, something is not being done right or emotions are getting in the way. I have seen boundaries effectively implemented in jails, acute psychiatry units, residential homes and ordinary homes, and for diverse problems ranging from anxiety disorders to psychotic disorders, from substance abuse disorders to serious disruptive behaviour disorders, and for the intellectually and socially impaired.

The step-by-step approach I outline below includes some specific advice about creating helpful boundaries. But I can't stress enough that before you try to 'manage' and contain your child, you must understand them first. You need to:

1. See the value of having these rules, and set aside enough time and energy to implement them – whatever it takes. And I do mean 'whatever it takes'. Any values, rules and consequences you develop have to be important enough to warrant the energy, patience and tolerance their implementation requires from you, your partner and your children. The adults will need each other to go the distance, and to present a united front to the children. Children will sense if there is any wavering or disunity, and will take advantage of any split to escape through the cracks.
2. Agree that *everyone* should live according to the values, rules and consequences set up for the family. Hypocrisy is toxic to effective boundaries, and makes enforcement of them so much harder. As an example, you wouldn't have a rule about swearing if one of the parents cursed frequently.
3. Spend time together (without the children) to discuss what you believe the values, rules and consequences should be. Parents *must* be united before involving the rest of the family.
4. Ensure there is enough playfulness, fun, acceptance, curiosity and affection in your family life. Boundaries without care = jail.

This strategy works best when children are at school age because they will be better able to understand the discussion process and to actually read the rules. Also, many classrooms use the same approach when developing discipline, so discipline at home and school will be united. The values-based approach still works with preschoolers, but will be more imposed and less negotiated.

Developing a united set of values

To create a new approach to boundaries requires a significant change in everyone's minds about how the family functions. In general I've found it useful to have a regular family meeting time. A weekly family discussion can keep the momentum going for addressing difficult things that otherwise might easily be postponed, avoided or blown over.

Consistency is important. Psychotherapy, Alcoholics Anonymous and Weight Watchers all work best when attended weekly. When I see children or parents for support it can be done infrequently and irregularly, but when I see people for specific change I usually insist on it being weekly. You should expect no less for your family if you truly want change. Here is one suggested outline for a series of weekly meetings to develop your values:

Week 1: Preparation
Week 2: Brainstorming values (what we want)
Week 3: Choosing 'our values'
Week 4: Brainstorming rules (what we don't want) and consequences (what it will take to make breaking the rules not worthwhile)
Week 5: Choosing and testing our rules and consequences
Week 6 onwards: Review and change

Week 1: Preparation

The first meeting should be scheduled at a time everyone will be able to attend each week, and not in response to a transgression – the aim is to try to make it a positive experience for the family. You might bring it up in the following way: 'Your mum/dad and I want us all to get together to think about what kind of family we want. So for the next couple of months we're all going to get together at seven o'clock on Mondays to work on it. Have a think about what kind of family you want us to be, and we'll talk about it Monday.'

It is possible that your children will be negative about the process, especially the older they are. Handle this with playfulness ('Let's see how it goes'), with acceptance ('It's okay that you aren't sure about this new thing'), with curiosity ('I wonder why you are so against this?') and with empathy ('It's not easy to do new things, honey'). Try not to talk about the forthcoming meeting for the rest of the week. If they bring up ideas, acknowledge them, but suggest they save further discussion for the meeting so everyone gets to hear what they think.

Week 2: Brainstorming values

First ask if anyone wants to take notes of everyone's ideas, and that at this stage all ideas will be accepted. Depending on the age of the children, it's likely that no one will put their hand up, so be prepared to do the job yourself. But if someone does put their hand up go with it as much as you can.

Going around in a circle one idea at a time, invite people to say what kind of family and place they want to live in. To get the ball rolling, give a couple of your own. For example:

- 'I want to live in a home where we are all safe.'
- 'I want to live in a family where my privacy is respected.'

For the next ten or fifteen minutes, let all family members brainstorm. All the ideas are to be written down, without censoring or correcting them (or rolling your eyes which is an unspoken criticism) no matter how ridiculous they seem to you. The following week the family will go through all the ideas and together choose the ones that they want and together reject the ridiculous ones.

Children (and some adults) usually struggle with this process, finding it easier to complain about what they *don't* want. For example:

- 'I don't want my brother to hit me.'
- 'I don't want people walking into my room anytime they want.'

- 'I don't want people using my things.'
- 'I don't want to be nagged all the time.'
- 'I don't want you reading my diary/looking at my Facebook page.'

If this happens, gently guide them by explaining, 'That is what you *don't* want. Tonight we are focusing on what we *do* want. How can you turn that around so it talks about what we do want?'

- 'I don't want to be hit' becomes 'I want to feel safe.'
- 'I don't want people to enter my room' becomes 'I want my privacy respected.'
- 'I don't want people using my things' becomes 'I want my things to be cared for.'

Some examples of values that families come up with include:

- I want people to be honest.
- I want people to care for me.
- I want people to respect my things.
- I want to be respected.
- I want to feel safe.
- I want things to be fair.
- I want to be listened to.
- I want the house to be peaceful.
- I want to be able to sleep without being woken up.
- I want pocket money.
- I want privacy.

Type up (or write up) the list and give a copy to each family member to think about before the next meeting. This may feel a bit formal (and be time-consuming!) but it is an important step as it helps everyone to feel some ownership of the ideas – less 'my values' and more 'our values'.

Handling negative responses

At this point, children's responses can vary from enthusiastic acceptance to mocking rejection. Whatever the response, accept it. You can't make your children engage in this process and if they wish to reject it they will. In fact, it is useful if they do reject it as there will be a logical consequence to their lack of involvement: they don't get a say in developing the family values that will lead to the rules and consequences. Initially, they may say, 'This is stupid. I'm not doing this!' But when they see you mean it and they start complaining about the rules and the costs associated with breaking them, you can simply remind them that they can always come to the weekly meeting and have their say then.

Lucas

Sixteen-year-old Lucas was often complaining, demanding and criticising, and spent much of his time on the computer playing on-line games yelling and swearing. His parents were exasperated with his rude and obnoxious behaviour and came to me for help.

Lucas refused to come and see me (saying it was his parents' problem, not his) so I discussed the idea of values-based rules with his parents. They worked very hard to get a united understanding of their son's behaviour and to learn how to manage it.

When Lucas was told about the meeting and that he was invited, he responded, 'That is *so* gay. You can't make me come to that!' The father responded, 'We have no intention of forcing you, Lucas. You're invited, but only come if you want to have a say in how our family is going to work from now on.'

Lucas didn't quite know how to respond to his father not getting involved in a fight with him over this, and just walked away.

The first brainstorming meeting was held: no Lucas.

The second meeting where the values were chosen was held: no Lucas. Those present wanted a peaceful house. This was written up and put on the fridge for all to see.

The third meeting where consistently broken rules were talked about and rules made was held – no Lucas. Those present decided that there would be no yelling or swearing in the house. This was written up and put on the fridge for all to see.

The fourth meeting where consequences for broken rules were

decided was held – no Lucas. Those present decided that any yelling or swearing that bothered others would result in the immediate disconnection of the Internet until the yelling or swearing stopped. This was written up and put on the fridge for all to see.

The following week was a firecracker!

The usual events occurred the first night, with Lucas yelling and swearing. The father simply walked to the router and turned off the Internet connection. Further swearing immediately followed and ten minutes later Lucas emerged from his room, went to check the Internet and found it was switched off and turned it back on.

'Who the #^@* turned it off?! I was in the middle of a game!' The father simply said, 'I did.' Lucas was furious and demanded to know why, to which the father said, 'It's what we decided at the meeting. A copy is on the fridge. Go check it out.'

'I didn't agree to this!'

'No, you weren't there.'

'Don't do it again!'

'We will until next week's meeting. It's our rule until then. If someone is yelling or swearing, the Internet goes off until it stops.'

At this point Lucas started yelling again. His father walked past him and calmly turned the connection off again.

'What did you do that for?!'

'You were yelling, so it goes off. When you stop, it goes on.'

Lucas stormed off to his room, yelling and swearing as he went, and when he stopped, his father switched it back on again.

Over the next week, every time someone was bothered by someone else's yelling or swearing, the Internet was turned off. Gradually the swearing lessened, until eventually if a swear word popped out, Lucas would quickly cry out, 'Don't turn it off! I'm in the middle of a good game!'

Lucas was invited to their next meeting and this time he attended. He argued strongly for a change in the cost. 'I just can't help swearing sometimes when I'm playing, but I don't want to lose my spot in the game.' This was the beginning of a conversation about his behaviour and a compromise between Lucas and his parents.

Week 3: Choosing 'our values'

At this meeting the family chooses the values that they all agree on. Now, to enable everyone to get a say, and to discuss pros and cons, may take more than fifteen minutes and perhaps require a couple of meetings.

During this time the ridiculous or harmful values are addressed, but rather than being criticised as stupid, they are simply not agreed to. For example, it would be hard to convince others of the benefit of 'everyone being able to do whatever they want' simply because the repercussions would be disastrous for everyone (e.g. a father spending the family savings on an expensive car, a mother gambling away the grocery money). If the creator of the inappropriate value storms off, let them go as they then have to pay the cost of having no say. And if all the children storm off then the parents have free rein until they return.

Taking an open and playful approach can help avoid conflict, and if the children are responding well, you can let them take more responsibility for this part of the process. In many situations I have found that children come up with really appropriate and salient values, and because they have initiated them they have a more powerful effect. In any case, it is difficult for them to disagree with ideas like 'our family should care, trust and respect each other and provide enough money, clothes, outings, freedom', and so on.

Allowing children more say helps them own the process, so they will be more open to accepting the subsequent rules and consequences. Another plus is that your children may start to internalise the values as their own thoughts – 'I'm agreeing to this not because my parents tell me, but because I think it is a good idea.'

Handling negative responses

If your children say, 'I don't care', accept their response. As explained above, they will soon learn the consequences of not being involved in this process. Meanwhile, your response could be something like: 'Okay, so you don't want to have a say in this and you're happy for us to make the decision for you? We can do that. We just thought that at your age you would have an opinion and would like a say about what kind of family you'd like to live in.'

If they then say, 'This is stupid!' or 'This is boring!' your response could be something like, 'Well we think having a safe family is pretty important, but thanks for letting us know what you think.'

And if your children say, 'I want to live in an unsafe house!', your response could be something like, 'Oh. That doesn't quite make sense to me. You'll have to explain the advantages of living in an unsafe house.' Rather than *you* defending the value, it becomes their job to justify their reasons for wanting their particular value. And since they won't be able to give convincing reasons why, for example, it's a good idea to risk being terrified, robbed, injured or even dying, they won't get other family members to agree with them.

In my experience, there are four values that cover most of those generated by the brainstorm at the first meeting.

1. We want to be safe.
2. We care for each other.
3. We care for our things.
4. We are all improving.

If children bring up other values, try to incorporate their ideas in their own words as this helps them to own the value. If you can, give their values a go for a week and then review them as a family, even if they are not what you would choose.

Sam

Sam, an only child aged fifteen, claimed he didn't care if the family improved or not. He was refusing to improve himself by attending school regularly or doing homework, and would not engage with any form of therapy to create change, saying, 'Just leave me alone'. He was not depressed or psychotic, just very stubborn and oppositional.

Sam's parents were at the end of their tether, and in a playful and accepting way decided to go with his expressed value of not wanting to improve, with the logical consequence of the *whole* family not improving. They moved all the electronic equipment into storage along with all the games, luxury items and expensive clothes. They even emptied the fridge and pantry of all the usual delicacies, replacing them with plain label items that one could expect to afford on an unemployment allowance. Mobile phone connections were put on hold so they could not be used.

The logical consequence of the family value of not caring or improving was that the family would have to live in poverty. It was unreasonable for Sam to refuse to do anything, yet still expect his parents to work hard and earn money to provide him with his computer, Internet, phone, clothes and pocket money.

It took four weeks, but grudgingly the son agreed that he wanted to live in a family where people were improving themselves. All the benefits of 'improvement' were gradually returned as his engagement in life and education increased.

The link between values and rules

Most school-aged children will be aware that if they agree to the values on the previous page, then they can be held to those values (as you can). For this reason, you can expect significant resistance – especially since one value covers a thousand rules. For example, if they agree they want to be cared for, this has implications for how they treat others including don't hit, don't swear at others, don't tease or put down, don't ignore or take for granted, don't walk in and turn the TV channel over, don't leave all the dishes for one person, don't be selfish with the things you have etc. If they don't want to be mistreated or randomly abused, then there is a family expectation that they won't mistreat or abuse others.

In the same way, if they agree to the value 'we want to be safe', this has implications for their behaviour inside and outside the home: what parties they can attend, what peer groups parents will support them seeing, what time they need to be home, whether they can climb on the roof, when they can ride their bike to school alone, when they can have a sleepover etc.

If they agree they want their things cared for, this has implications for how they treat others' possessions including asking to borrow them (rather than simply taking them), accepting 'no' as an answer, being careful with another's possessions, and taking on their share of chores that look after the whole family's 'things' such as cleaning rooms, hanging towels, putting away clothes, washing dishes or helping in the garden. If they want their favourite jeans washed or their laptop keyboard to work properly (without sticky food in the keys), then there is a family expectation that they will take care of others' things too.

And if they agree that everyone should be improving, this implies that children accept having to go to school and do homework, adults getting the best job they can for their family (not necessarily the best paid) and that the family will support their own and each others' goals by getting a good night's sleep, keeping the noise down, staying off phones and Internet after a certain time etc. And if someone is sick and it impacts on their earning or learning, their 'sick role' is to do everything possible to get well, whether it is going to bed early, taking medication, going to counselling or losing weight by eating nutritious low-calorie foods and exercising regularly. If children expect their parent to go to work and earn money so the family is not homeless and they get to have good things like bikes, computers, presents, books, holidays, and nice clothes, then the family would expect them to get well, go to school, do their best, and not sit up late surfing the Internet and then say they are too tired to go to school.

As you can see, it is much easier to talk about and agree on what you want as a family, than on what you don't want. And once all family members agree (or at least don't reasonably disagree) on those values, the values underpin any decisions around boundaries, as anything that breaks those values becomes a target for change. Thus the rules and consequences we are going to add are not arbitrary but have a clear and positive purpose.

Once the values are agreed to, they should be 'externalised' – printed out, signed by all and put somewhere prominent in the house. They then become 'our values'.

For some families, the weekly meetings can decrease in frequency from here as the family lives according to the agreed values. When unwanted behaviour occurs, the parent simply reminds the child of the values that the family agreed to. In many cases the child is well aware of what is appropriate, and extended explanations are not necessary or even helpful. However, where there is consistent, unacceptable 'value breaking', rules and consequences may need to be added to the values, and you move to the next step.

Week 4: Brainstorming rules and consequences

The next family meeting is focused on developing rules and consequences to go with any values that are consistently and problematically ignored. It is at this point that family members get to say what they *don't* want (the rules) and what it would take to stop the rules being broken (the consequences). As before, a brainstorming session is recommended, with all complaints and potential solutions written down and no criticism or attempt made to decide on what is a helpful or unhelpful idea at this point. Everyone takes away a copy and is encouraged to think about what they don't want and what they think it would take to prevent it. Once again, keep the meeting short. Most problems have been around for months if not years, so although there is understandably a wish to immediately fix them all in one go, dragging out a meeting to try to cover everything just makes it more likely that tempers will fray and prevent change from happening. As much as possible, keep it simple.

Week 5: Choosing and testing rules and consequences

The following week, the family tries to reach consensus on what is not wanted in their family and what consequences will apply. Consequences should be linked with a rule, and every rule linked with a value. As far as possible go with what the children bring up, even if it is not exactly what you would have chosen. It does not matter what the rules and consequences are, as they can be reviewed and changed each week. A 'silly' rule or consequence can be helpful as it won't work and this is a good experience for the children to see that they were taken seriously, and that rules can be altered until they are 'helpful'.

And if a consequence is too light, its severity can be increased weekly until its strength makes the rule not worth breaking.

Once the rules and consequences are agreed to, pick one (two at the most) to implement the following week. As with the 'values', externalise the rules and consequences by writing them on a piece of paper and put them in a prominent place (make a couple of copies in case they are scribbled on or even ripped up!). If you don't think it necessary to write them down, make them into a statement that is easy to remember, and that each family member can accurately repeat. These rules and consequences become the law until reviewed the week after. They cannot be altered, the adults *must* implement the consequences without fail and in the agreed way, and any complaints about the rules or consequences have to be saved for the next weekly meeting. The children will often want to talk about how unfair or how stupid it all is during the week, particularly at the time when the consequences are being implemented. When they do this, accept their opinion, even playfully thank them for letting you know, and simply direct them in a broken record fashion to bring up their concerns at the next family meeting, 'But until then, this is how it is going to be.'

Some examples of values-based boundaries		
Value	**Rule**	**Consequence**
We are safe	Don't return late	We'll be picked up early
We care for people	Don't hit	No TV for one day
We care for things	Put dirty clothes in laundry	Do own washing
We improve	Homework must be done	No games until done
Peaceful house	No yelling inside	Yellers go outside

Rules work best if they can be measured

Don't choose a rule that involves an attitude, as judging whether a transgression has occurred can itself cause an argument. For example, avoid rules like: 'Don't have a bad attitude', 'Don't be disrespectful',

'Don't be slack with homework', 'Don't be lazy', 'Don't watch too much TV.' These are subjective and mostly immeasurable, so the child can then simply deny what they are being accused of. Instead, keep rules connected to objective and measurable events such as specific behaviours like yelling, hitting and swearing; the completion of tasks like homework or chores; and specified times spent on activities such as the Internet or TV.

Week 6 onwards: Review and change

From then on, the first few minutes of each family meeting can be set aside for reviewing the previous week and discussing any concerns about the existing values, rules and consequences. These can be changed, left alone or removed, and new rules and consequences can be added as required. I'd suggest meeting weekly for at least two months until it's clear to the children that you are serious as a family about meeting the agreed values. If everything is running well, you can decrease the duration and frequency of the meeting, or increase it if the values start being broken again.

In general, the fewer rules and consequences you have, the more effective they will be. Try to have only one or at most two new rules and consequences at any one time; pick what is most important or most achievable to work on first. As we have seen, values are generally more powerful than rules, and also broader reaching. Being values-focused also keeps in everyone's minds what we all want to be, and is a more positive approach to setting boundaries than reeling off a list of what is not wanted and how the person is perceived as not measuring up. Consider the difference between, 'I hope you have a great day at school today. Remember to be kind', versus, 'I hope you don't get into trouble today. And stop lying to the other kids or they won't want to play with you.' It's pretty obvious which approach is more likely to lead to the young person feeling better about themselves, and therefore to encourage more positive behaviour.

Try (as much as is possible and practical) to keep the making and implementing of values, rules and consequences playful rather than serious. The more serious it is (and as we saw in Chapter 4, seriousness suggests that there is only one way to do something), the more shame your child will feel when they don't measure up, and the more disappointment and anger we will feel when values are broken. The anger that shame generates will either be self-directed, or directed at those nearest them; neither response being particularly helpful at helping them to think, reflect and learn.

When children make mistakes, say something like, 'Oh, well. We can always try again tomorrow.' Expressions like this are vital for children to experience, as they let them know that mistakes can be accepted, forgiveness is possible, things can be repaired, and more importantly, if things don't work out as planned, it is not the end of the world. They are still in trouble for breaking the rules, but there is less negative emotion from their parents, and the consequence given is not personal, it is simply 'the law' and it is predictable: 'Oh well, honey, you know what happens now.'

SETTING EFFECTIVE CONSEQUENCES

It would be so easy if all we had to do was make a rule and it was obeyed – if only the process of simply agreeing on the rule was enough to get your child to live within the boundary. But since our children are not us and they have to develop and work it out for themselves (one of the tasks of childhood is to *test* boundaries) it is more than likely that family rules will be broken. When it happens, having a consequence that you have already agreed to is an enormous help, as you are less likely to be emotional and reactive (you know the scenario: banning or grounding the child for a ridiculous period of time, shouting, or resorting to smacking).

Ultimately, the idea of setting consequences is to help children learn self-control, rather than always needing you to do the controlling. Every time we step in and tell them what to do or make them do something (us saving them), we may achieve some control over their behaviour, but our children miss out on a valuable experience to gain self-control: i.e. choosing for themselves and dealing with the outcome of that choice.

Here are seven ways to ensure consequences are more effective in helping build a child's self-control:

1 Allow children to devise and test consequences

First up, let me be clear that parents have the final say; a family is not a democracy. The participants are not equal (except the parents) and each member does not have equal rights and responsibilities. If the parents don't sign off on a value, rule or consequence, it doesn't happen. Though we want to support our children, we are not going to be negligent and will step in and save them if their decisions are seriously flawed or dangerous.

As an example, fifteen-year-olds won't be provided alcohol at their birthday party, no matter how much they want it or threaten, 'We'll get it anyway.' And if alcohol turns up at the party, the drinkers go home or the party is cancelled, no matter how much your child begs. As adults we know that if a fifteen-year-old and their peers can't have a good party without alcohol, they are at risk of suffering serious difficulties in the coming years. We will not support decisions like those, and will 'save' the fifteen-year-olds by stepping in and telling them what to do, with clear consequences if the boundaries are broken. Though we accept they will possibly try to get around this, we are not going to give them permission to get around it.

Having said that, it is wise to let your children initiate and lead as much as you consider safe and reasonable, as this will increase their sense of ownership of the developed rules and consequences. My experience is that when children own this process, they often choose consequences that are appropriate and at least as restrictive as ones we would choose. Here is an example one twelve-year-old came up with:

Value: We spend time together.

Rule: We all eat dinner together if we are in the house.

Consequence: I don't get to contact my friends that night.

Developing values, rules and consequences creates a balance between supporting and saving your child, in parenting them and letting them parent themselves. What I am suggesting is that all things being equal and safe enough, err on the side of support and go with what your children wish to try. If their ideas don't work, you can always change them later. So asking them, 'What do you think would be a good enough consequence?' or 'What's it going to take for you to not do that again?' is often a good first step. If they don't come up with anything, then you get to choose.

2 Use logical consequences

There are numerous situations where a consequence logically follows on from the unwanted behaviour. As much as possible allow the logical outcome to direct what the consequence is.

- If you punch a wall you will be in pain.
- If you treat your friends badly they will avoid you.
- If you lie to your parents they will trust you less.
- If you are caught stealing from a shop the police will be called.
- If you don't turn up to football practice you won't be picked for the team.
- If you perform badly at work you will not be promoted or will be fired.

No parent wants to see their children suffer because of their bad decisions, and forgiveness and second chances are important. However, if we regularly or excessively save our children from the logical consequences of their actions, we may be harming the development of their decision-making. Their having to deal with bad outcomes is an important learning experience.

However, you need to remember that supporting them requires acceptance and empathy. You can still be on their side and caring of them even when you don't step in to fix the problem for them. If your children believe that you could fix it but won't, they're likely to be annoyed at you, so you need to be confident about it being okay that they miss out and suffer, and be able to tolerate their disappointment and anger.

Value: We respect and look after our possessions.
Rule: We don't damage our possessions.
Consequence: Toys that are damaged won't work.

A logical consequence

A teenage boy when arguing with his mother called her a 'f---ing bitch' and then stormed off to his room. An hour later he came out and told her that they had to leave for sports practice. The mother replied, 'Oh, are you talking to me? I'm confused; 'f---ing bitches' don't usually help other people. That's what mums do for their kids. When you work out whether I am a 'f---ing bitch' or a mum, let me know.'

The boy experienced the logical consequence of treating someone in a nasty way. And the mum showed a remarkably playful and calm approach in accepting his comments, but explaining the consequences involved. When the boy realised that the only way to repair the situation was to apologise, he apologised and then got what he wanted.

3 Use immediate consequences

Try to avoid consequences that come into effect a day or more after a rule is broken, especially with young or emotional children whose understanding of future events is usually poor. A consequence that will happen sometime in the future will be ineffectual in curbing their current behaviour because compared to the strong emotion they are feeling now, the potential consequence hardly exists. A few hours or days after the event, the unwanted behaviour is over, but the consequence then kicks in, and to their emotional brain the cost is completely unconnected to the original behaviour.

We want to directly connect the rules to an immediate outcome if possible. If someone is screaming, they go outside until they stop. If someone is arguing in the car, the car immediately pulls over until the argument stops. If siblings are fighting and can't sort it out themselves, they are separated and sent to their rooms.

The advantage of a one-day limit is that each morning is a new day, and you and your child can try again with a clean slate. The past can be left where it belongs – in the past.

Value: We are all safe.

Rule: No one hits or threatens to hit someone in our family.

Consequence: No screen time (including TV, computer, mobile, iPod and electronic games) for twenty-four hours.

4 Start with smaller consequences

Don't go straight to the most severe consequence (though this is always tempting when we are angry ourselves – one reason why writing down the rules and costs can help). Make the initial one relatively small, but with the clear message that it will increase in severity until the rule is followed. For example, if a child refuses to turn the sound down on his computer game or the TV, he must stop playing/watching it for ten seconds (get him to count to ten) and then he gets a second chance. If he turns it up again, he cannot play or watch for thirty seconds. The next time it is one minute. Then five minutes. Then fifteen minutes. Then he doesn't get to continue the activity until the next day.

Also, don't immediately go to the thing that is most important to them. Start with simple things and leave the more potent things for later. This gives them a chance to rein themselves in with a relatively minor consequence (with relatively minor frustration), but knowing that if they don't back down a more significant consequence will be invoked. For example, access to social networking sites is a strong motivator for some teenagers and easy to block by simply turning off the modem, turning off the power, or turning off the fuse box if necessary. So though this could ultimately be used, you would try to use less potent motivators before pulling out the 'big guns'. The message is, 'We will do whatever it takes. We'd rather the consequences be small, but we will increase them until the rules are met. How far we have to go is totally up to you.'

5 Don't use consequences that restrict development

Avoid consequences that interfere with their development, such as missing out on a sporting event, dancing class, camp or other school activity, or seeing relatives or important attachment figures. There are many other options that can be used that don't have any developmental implications such as TV, music, Internet, mobile phones, social networking sites (though, of course, many would argue these are vital for their development!), toys, games, new clothes, make-up and pocket money.

6 Make consequences apply to all

Hypocrisy is toxic to boundaries; consistency reinforces them. If 'yellers go outside' and a parent finds himself yelling, he needs to take himself outside until he has calmed down. Watch the children's amazed response if you do this.

If 'swearers must go to a time-out room', watch what happens when the parent puts herself in time-out for swearing. It becomes not only an example of justice, but the parent can make a playful joke of her infraction, apologise for breaking the rule, and therefore model repair (getting over the problem with a minimum of shame).

7 Match consequences to maturity

We expect more care of a house from an adult than a child, so chores are divided according to age. A five-year-old only has to tidy his toys up. A ten-year-old has to keep her room clean. A fifteen-year-old has to iron. A parent has to clean bathrooms.

We also expect more self-restraint from an adult. A three-year-old hitting with a fist may result in a brief time-out. A nine-year-old hitting with a fist may result in the loss of screen time for twenty-four hours; a thirteen-year-old being grounded for a week; but a twenty-year-old hitting with a fist may result in an assault charge or being made to leave home. A parent hitting with a fist may result in an assault charge or intervention from child protection.

If there is a broad age range of siblings, uniform consequences may not be appropriate. The consequence could then be altered according to the age of each family member. For example:

Value: We care for each other.

Rule: No swearing at others.

Consequence: Swearers have to pay per word: 50c if under 10; $1 if aged 11–15 and $10 for parents.

Such provisos according to age allow the opportunity to talk about 'rights and responsibilities' within the family. Though children have less responsibility and the adults more, children also have less freedom and the adults more. As children age their freedoms increase, but so too do their responsibilities.

Never ask 'why'

When deciding whether a rule has been broken, and whether to implement consequences, in the heat of the moment never ask 'why' a child performed the unwanted action, as they will then proceed to give you numerous excuses in an effort to deflect the consequences. Only ask 'what' they did. Once the consequences have played out and the reptilian brain is soothed and mammalian brain is secured, you can then explore the 'why' together with your human brains as you make sense and create a story of what happened and why.

Ask what, not why

Ten-year-old Emily has hit her younger sister, Eva. Their father heard the fight, and knows from Eva's tears and Emily's indignation that emotions are still running high. If he asks why it happened, here's how the exchange might sound:

Dad: Emily, why did you hit Eva?
Emily: Well, she called me names.
Dad: Eva, why did you call her names?
Eva: [still crying] She took my DS!
Dad: Why did you take her DS?
Emily: I didn't take her DS!
Eva: Yes, you did!
Emily: No, I didn't! Anyway, you took my scooter yesterday!

And around, and around it goes.

By way of comparison, consider the following exchange:

Dad: Emily, what did you do?

Emily: She called me names!

Dad: That may be so, but what did you do?

Emily: But she always takes my things!

Dad: That may be so, but what did you do?

Emily: You always take her side.

Dad: We need to sort this out first. What did you do?

Emily: I hit her.

Dad: And what happens to people in our house who hit others?

Emily: They go to their rooms.

Dad: So you know what to do. I'll come and get you in ten minutes and we can talk more about it then.

The father's 'broken record' approach (repeatedly asking 'What did you do?'), and having a clear rule and boundary allows him to stay out of the fight between the girls and to simply implement the consequence. The question 'why' was going to be addressed, but only after the consequence was out of the way, and hopefully at a time when the girls' minds were able to reflect on what happened.

CHAPTER 10

REFLECT MORE, REACT LESS

So far we have looked at providing a safe place for children to live, where basic needs are met, where the adults are united, where there is enough care and affection, and where there is a balance between freedom and containment. When 'enough' of each of these is provided for your children, you are maximising their healthy social and emotional development.

However, there is one final aspect of parenting that is unique to humans: mirroring or reflecting the child's 'self'. Reflecting requires us to be 'in tune' with our children, to be with them as they are without trying to control them – something we can't do if we are preoccupied. It requires us to see our children as separate to ourselves rather than as an extension of ourselves, and to interact with them as they are rather than as we wish them to be. Reflecting also requires us to be mindful of our own feelings – to 'observe', understand and restrain them. For, as we have seen throughout this book, it is emotion that makes parenting (indeed any relationship) so tricky at times. The emotions are not right or wrong, good or bad, they are simply telling us something. They need to be understood and accepted, not fought or denied.

Broadly speaking, there are three ways we can interact with our children when intense emotions are involved: reacting, responding and reflecting. Reacting is the most normal response (we all do it, usually as if we are on autopilot), but is not always the most helpful response to our children's emotions. By learning to respond and reflect more, we can help our children (and ourselves) develop the ability to manage challenging emotions such as rage and deep sadness.

REACTING (taking on their emotion)

In this first approach, you react to your child's emotions by becoming emotional yourself.

Where does that intense emotion come from?

Many of us know what it's like to be feeling relaxed and calm and to suddenly fly off the handle when our child says or does something provocative. What's interesting is that the emotion is not always coming from us. Let's examine this in more detail.

The emotion may be coming from you

There are any of a number of personal reasons for becoming emotional (tiredness, illness, stress or the accidental triggering of negative thought patterns), but whatever the reason, your emotion may be quite unrelated to anything your child may have said or done, and is *your own issue* to deal with. It is therefore inappropriate to blame your child, or to take it out on them.

If you find yourself feeling anxious, angry or sad whenever your child expresses her own emotions, you need to develop your own emotion regulation skills – after all, if we want our children to manage their emotions better, we need to lead the way.

The emotion may be coming from your child

Your child at times is 'filled up' by emotions that are hard to bear such as anger, sadness, worry, or insecurity. When this happens, their emotional brain (mammalian and reptilian brain combined) is activated and mobilises its defences to cope.

But if these strategies are inadequate because the emotion is too overwhelming or the coping strategies are too weak, your child becomes 'mindless' and seeks out relief. Beginning in infancy, a child's most effective way of coping with overwhelming emotions is to make them *your* problem and to get you to deal with the situation that caused them. This is commonly done by provoking in the parent the powerful emotions the child feels in themselves, and being able to say, 'I'm not the angry one, you're the angry one' (this is known as projection). Such provocation can be achieved in various ways including statements such as 'I hate you', actions such as rolling their eyes, or provocative questions such as 'Why can't I have another ice-cream?'

The parents' immediate response to a provocation is often emotional. If the parents' thoughtful human brain is unable to restrain or leash their own initial emotional responses, like their children they, too, fill up and become overwhelmed by their emotions.

As your child experiences you filling up with emotion, her own emotion and discomfort often settles. When projection (dumping and seeing your own emotions in someone else as a way of coping with them) is occurring, the more the parent 'loses it', the calmer the child often becomes. Have you ever noticed how, after you have seriously lost it due to provocation, your child sometimes becomes remarkably calm and well behaved? She is no longer feeling angry, sad, worried, insecure, powerless, hopeless or worthless because her emotions have been transferred to you.

Projecting and off-loading responsibility for emotional problems are primitive and completely unconscious ways of coping. Your child does not sit there thinking, 'I'm feeling angry, so I'm going to provoke Dad to fury, which means I can both punish him as well as make *him* the angry one, not me.' Rather, your child has discovered through years of trial and error that provoking an emotion in his parent soothes his own discomfort. He doesn't know why it works or why he does it and is not likely to be aware that he is doing it. Asking him, 'Why are you provoking me like this?' will usually be met with 'I don't know' or 'What are you talking about?'

Though reacting to your child's emotions is generally unhelpful, don't be upset with yourself if you do. Reacting is a very normal, immediate and understandable response to provocation, and is sometimes quite appropriate. You are not a robot, you are a mammal, and we can all be overwhelmed by provocation. It's important that your children see you experience emotions and then 'get over them' (though if you lose all control and become mindless, there is little advantage in this).

You can be sure that your child's peers will almost certainly react to any provocation your child gives them, and most people in their life (including most adults) will respond to emotional provocation by reacting.

The disadvantages of reacting

1. It lets them off the hook. The emotions your child feels are *their* emotions, not yours. It is their developmental task to learn how to deal with them, not yours. If the child gets rid of their uncomfortable emotions through us, they may not learn new and more mature ways of coping with the distress caused by sadness, anger, worry or insecurity.
2. It teaches your child to provoke more. They learn that it works to provoke you or other adults. So every time you react, you are making it more likely that they will provoke again.
3. It is uncomfortable. When you react, your thinking brain tends to switch off or be less influential. You may do and say things that you later regret, and it is not a good feeling to be out of control.

How to handle reacting

- Don't beat yourself up. Accept what happened, forgive yourself, and repair it.
- As quickly as you can soothe your reptilian rage or anger (go for a quick walk, have a cup of tea, cuddle a pet), secure your mammalian insecurity (perhaps call your partner and talk it through together), and reflect on and make sense of what is going on with your human brain.

- Apologise if you need to ('Sorry, Charlie, I was furious but I don't want to yell and scream like that. That's not the kind of dad I want to be').
- When you and your child are calm enough, discuss what happened and address any consequences.
- Always repair the situation. It's tempting when things are calmer to 'let sleeping dogs lie' and not talk about what happened. However, if the cause of the reaction is not repaired and resolved, it is more likely to be repeated. (As we saw in Chapter 9, if getting you to react means children avoid a consequence, you have just taught them to provoke you again next time.)

RESPONDING (leaving the emotion with them)

In this second approach, rather than reacting to your children's emotions by becoming emotional yourself, you restrain your own emotions and calmly respond to their provocation. Let's look at how this may work.

As above, your child is filled up by a difficult emotion (insecurity, anger, sadness, worry), her more mature strategies don't work well enough to manage it, and she becomes overwhelmed. To cope, your child tries to provoke you so that you take on her difficult emotion, and you begin to feel it rising up in you.

However, at this point (unlike reacting) you recognise that the emotion you are feeling is coming from your child, and you know that by taking it on, you deny her the opportunity to develop her own emotion regulation. So rather than reacting you 'respond' to your child's emotion by calmly answering her provocative question, statement or action.

A visual image may help when trying to keep your cool under pressure. Imagine a brick wall between you and your child that keeps the projected emotion on her side of the wall. Unable to off-load her tricky emotions, the child is left with the discomfort on her side, and has two options: either to increase her provocation in an attempt to break down your brick wall and get you to react, or to work out another way of coping – hopefully a more mature one. This is an important moment. If by increasing her provocation and upping the ante your child does break the wall down and you react rather than respond, you have inadvertently taught her to provoke *more* as a way of coping with her difficult emotions – a very unhelpful outcome for everyone.

But a child will only hit his head against a brick wall for so long before he gets a headache. If this increased provocation does not result in you reacting, he will eventually give up and try a different way of coping.

Strengthening the 'brick wall'

If the 'brick wall' response is to be used, it is vital that it is strong enough to withstand the onslaught. A double brick wall (united mother and father) or even a triple or quadruple brick wall (parents united with a school and therapist) can assist in strengthening the wall against the predictable increase in attacks.

Having a pre-existing, predictable, externalised response (consequences) is another way of reinforcing the wall (see the previous chapter on boundaries). If the provocation breaks a rule such as 'no swearing', you can simply activate the consequence – swearing at you has only hurt your child, helping you to not get defensive or have hurt feelings. Many parents also find the 'broken record' technique useful, which is simply a repetitive response delivered calmly.

Children tend to be quite expert at provoking, and they often know our weak spots and triggers better than we know them ourselves. No brick wall is perfectly strong, and can fall down under enough pressure. If your wall does break down and you end up reacting as outlined earlier, don't beat yourself up – it is totally understandable. What needs to happen, though, is a rapid repair of the breach by calming yourself as soon as you can, acknowledging your mistake in reacting, adding reinforcements and united 'extra walls' if necessary, and going back to a responding approach and restating the agreed values, rules and consequences.

The power of the broken record

Teen: I want to go to the party.

Parent: We've talked about it and decided you can't go as there will be no parent at the house.

Teen: But Olivia's parents said it was okay for her to go.

Parent: You still can't go.

Teen: But everyone is going.

Parent: That may be so, but you still can't go.

Teen: Why are you so overprotective?!

Parent: You know our answer.

Teen: You don't care about me and what I want.

Parent: You know our answer.

Teen: I bet you went to parties like this when you were my age.

Parent: Whether I did or not is irrelevant. You can't go to this one.

Teen: So you did go to parties like this!

Parent: It doesn't matter what I did. We've decided you can't go to this party.

Teen: I hate you!

Parent: That's okay. Our answer hasn't changed.

Teen runs to the bedroom and slams the door.

The advantages of responding

1. You stay cool and calm, your mind is switched on, and you are able to maintain a positive, even playful attitude.
2. Your child (once they've stopped upping the ante) may learn new ways of coping, which will hopefully be more mature.
3. It is a more helpful way of interacting with your child at an emotional level.

The disadvantages of responding

1. Children are likely to escalate their provocations before they try other ways of coping. This requires you to be prepared and confident.

2 Responding can be hard work, as it requires you to be consistent, patient and controlled for long periods – a big ask. The temptation to try an easier and quicker way to deal with their emotions is always present. In the short term, reacting can be much easier and may feel more natural.
3 If your brick wall breaks down, it reinforces the escalating of provocation (the child unconsciously recognises 'It has worked!'), which makes it more likely that the child will escalate the next time.
4 Children can experience the broken record approach as proof that they are not on our mind ('You're not listening to me!), heightening their insecurity and leading to an increase in attachment behaviours. It can precipitate an emotional or behavioural crisis, and thus you will need to be clear and confident about how you will respond if your children lose it (see 'The Four Stage Plan' in Chapter 5).
5 The responding approach can actually be used in a punitive way where an adult angrily enforces the rules without listening to the child's perspective. You thus need to be aware of your own emotions when doing this as you may think you are 'responding' when in fact your underlying anger is making it more of a reaction.
6 The last disadvantage of responding to emotion is that it is often a waste of time. I would suggest that more than 90 per cent of the time our children know what our response to their question, statement or action will be and are just testing us or trying to get us to react. Do you really need to tell them that they can't have a second ice-cream, that they can't hit their brother, or that they have to do their homework?

   Mostly, they don't need a response as they already know what we think, and by responding we may be engaging in an unhelpful argument in which we are telling them what to do (saving them) rather than putting it back on them and making them responsible for themselves (supporting them). 'You'll work it out', 'I know you can do it', and 'I reckon you know what to do' are all ways of keeping 'their problem' their problem.

Of course, to maintain the balance there is the proviso, 'You can always ask; the answer may be yes or it may be no, but you can always ask.'

REFLECTING (giving the emotion back to them)

In this approach, you neither react to your children's emotions (becoming emotional yourself) nor respond to their emotions (enforcing a consequence or playing the broken record). Rather, you gently reflect their emotions back to them, along with your understanding of what is happening and why.

Next time you see a mother with an infant, take some time to watch how they interact together. While holding a happy and content baby, the mother looks happy, too, has a big smile on her face, and says things like, 'You're a happy baby now! Look at that big smile!' When the baby is sad, the mother feels some sadness too, her face looks a bit sad (though not as sad as the baby usually), and she says things like, 'Oh honey, you're not feeling so good.' And when the baby is grumpy or angry, the mother will have a slightly angry look on her face (again reflecting a modified version of the baby's anger), and says things like, 'Ooh! Baby is a bit angry at Mummy for not picking you up fast enough ... You're a bit cross at Mummy.'

Your baby cannot see themselves, but they see in your face a reflection of their feelings. As we saw in Chapter 1, mothers are a child's first mirror – helping them understand themselves. Winnicott described this process as becoming attuned to our child, whereby we gently show them who they are with our own face, body and emotional responses. The words used are less important in infancy, but as children grow our use of language to describe emotions becomes very valuable in their development of an emotional language.

Almost all parents reflect with their infants, so observing new mothers is a way of re-learning how to reflect emotions to your own children. I say this because some parents stop reflecting to their children, or have always struggled to reflect as they are too reactive. Reflecting is a human brain activity, and you won't be able to do it adequately if you are anxious or angry, depressed, avoidant, insecure, exhausted, distracted or intoxicated.

How reflecting works

When children experience strong feelings, they are often overwhelmed. As discussed in earlier chapters, their most basic and unconscious way of coping is to make their problem *our* problem. They learn to off-load their tricky emotion by provoking the emotion in us, usually through a question, statement or action. When they provoke us like this, we often find ourselves reacting – taking on their emotion – which escalates the drama, and makes it more likely that they'll use provocation in the future. However, even if we are able to restrain our emotions, and calmly respond by telling them what to do, we are still 'saving them'. It is better to try to support children to understand themselves and their own emotions. You do this by talking *with* them, not talking *at* them. You want your children to know you are thinking of them, that you have listened to what they have said (even if you don't agree with it), that you have made an attempt to understand where they are coming from, and that they and their needs are on your mind. In Chapter 1 we saw that children feel secure when they believe they are on your mind. 'Reflecting' clearly requires us to be thinking of the child and is thus a powerful attachment behaviour.

So you reflect on what is happening for your children to try to get some understanding about what is going on for them. You 'watch, wait and wonder' to try to imagine why they are behaving the way they are. And then you reflect back your understanding – a bit like holding up a mirror to show them what they look like but in this case your comments, facial expressions, gestures and actions are the mirror. The reflection you give back is simply a comment on what you have observed, and it is not harsh and unforgiving but instead modified by both your thoughtful wondering of what might be going on for your children, and your love for them.

So when reflecting, you:

- Use your thinking brain to be aware of and restrain your emotional brain so you either don't react or control your reaction.
- Think about your child's emotions and behaviours (as well as your own) and wonder what is going on in a moment of thoughtful silence.
- Offer a general comment naming the emotion and what it might be like for your child at that time. For example, 'I can see you are feeling pretty frustrated at the moment', or 'I can see you are really upset; it must be hard for you.'
- Make a specific comment on the nature and cause of the child's emotion. For example, after a child says, 'I hate you!' you might say, 'It seems like you become really angry when I don't do exactly what you want.'
- Wait for their response quietly. If their response involves further provocation such as, 'Oh, shut up! You're such a dick!' you might say, 'I wonder if you want to make me angry as well.'
- Finish off with a supportive comment suggesting that they can handle this situation – 'I know you can do this' – that you have confidence in them, and that they can always ask for help if they get stuck.

Note that in all of the above steps, you have not answered them or told them what to do. You have just commented on what it might be like for them, shown that you are trying to understand it from their point of view, and that you believe in them and their ability to work it out. You have not taken a 'serious' or stern approach, either. Instead, you are accepting of where the child is at and hopeful for change, not expecting them to be different right now.

Obviously, you would only reflect at those times when emotions are high or some provocation is occurring. If your child asks, 'Can you please pass the salt?' it would be ridiculous to reflect with, 'It seems you'd like me to pass you the salt.' But if the salt was right in front of them and they demanded, 'Give us the salt!', then you could react with, 'Get it yourself!', you could respond with, 'I'm not going to. You need to get it yourself', or you could reflect with, 'So even though the salt is right in front of you, you want me to get it for you.'

The three types of reflection

1 ***The adult reflects (thinks about the situation), but keeps their thoughts to themselves***

This is the key aspect of reflecting when emotions are involved, and is the core part of 'watch, wait and wonder'. This is almost always helpful, and if you are doing this you are probably not reacting (generally a good thing). It would only be a problem in those rare times when your child actually needs you to react; for example, if your child is drowning you don't sit there wondering how it happened or how he is feeling, you jump into the pool!

2 ***The adult reflects, names the emotion and provides a supportive statement***

'I wonder if you're feeling a bit angry/sad/worried. It must seem really unfair/it's hard to miss out/it's difficult to know what to do.'

Though you may have some understanding of what is happening and why, you keep those thoughts to yourself and simply let your child know you have seen his emotion (he is on your mind), and you have some empathy for his difficulty. Reflecting involves being with your child in his difficulty and not looking away; this takes great strength.

3 ***The adult reflects and offers a modified comment to help the child make sense of their thoughts and feelings***

Generally you would do this only occasionally – silent and supportive reflecting is usually enough to help your child feel secure, and also helps you to avoid reacting.

Not looking away

For nine months a father I know nursed his teenage daughter who had a brain tumour. She gradually lost her vision, her ability to move, control of her bowels, and finally her ability to eat and then breathe. She died in their home.

I remember visiting their house and seeing the outrageous suffering of this beautiful young girl, and experiencing the incredible drive to save her, and the helplessness at not being able to. And I remember wanting to look away, to not have to see her suffering and pain. If I couldn't fix it, it was hard to be there. Every time I turned up to visit, particularly as it became difficult for her to speak, the young girl would look me in the eye and hold my gaze. As I held her hand I forced myself to look into her eyes as if to say, 'I can see you. I won't look away. I can bear it with you, too.'

Her father did not look away and stayed with her through the horror of her illness with all its hope and grief and disappointment. I don't think I have ever witnessed such love and sacrifice. There was nothing he could do to save her, only support her and be with her. Someone asked at the funeral, 'How do you possibly get through such pain?' 'Together' is the only possible answer.

Modified versus unmodified reflections

In making comments about what your child is experiencing, it is important that you are not a cold, harsh or uncaring mirror. This is why I have used the word 'modified'. We don't mirror back exactly what we see as this could be experienced by the child as quite persecutory – as if we are showing them up or shaming them in their immaturity. (For example, it would be particularly cruel to record your child's tantrums on video and later play them back, especially if others are watching. While a video may be an accurate reflection – it really is what the child looked like – it is unmodified by care or love.)

Instead, we modify the reflection, being gentle with our language so our children are empowered rather than shamed. For example, if your child is struggling with jealousy of a more attractive sibling:

Unmodified reflection: 'You feel jealous that your sister is more attractive than you.'

Modified reflection: 'It's hard when someone close to you gets more attention and you feel left out.'

While the unmodified reflection may be true, it is cruel to say it in such a blunt way. The modified version is also true, but is less crushing, and lets your child know that you understand such a situation is not easy.

In summary, reflecting is your calm, thoughtful, playful, accepting, curious and loving observation of your child – your attempt (which will always be imperfect) to understand their emotions and behaviours, and to mirror or reflect that understanding back to your child in a modified and helpful way. In this way you share with your child their difficulties and say, 'I see you. I can bear it, too.'

The disadvantages of reflecting

If overused, reflecting can seem a bit wooden – as if you are 'trying to be a therapist' – though this is rarely a problem if you silently reflect. You would generally only use reflection when emotions are high and you feel you are being provoked. If your child shouted at you, 'By the way, you're the worst parent in the world!' then the reflection, 'I can see you are really angry with me at the moment', may help you keep control of your feelings and avoid getting sucked into an argument. But if your ten-year-old asks to stay up late on a school night, and the family rule states that bedtime is always 8.30 p.m., it would be a bit silly to reflect back, 'It seems you'd like to stay up late.' You'd simply respond and say, 'No. You know the rule.'

The advantages of reflecting

- You are able to stay calm and unprovoked in the face of high emotion, giving the message that strong feelings can be handled.
- Your child is given the opportunity to cope in more mature and thoughtful ways (rather than dumping the problem with you).
- You model words and ideas for your child to explain how and why they feel what they do.

- Because you are confident you are being reasonable, you don't need to defend yourself and get drawn into unnecessary arguments. You are simply rephrasing her question in a way that helps her understand herself.
- Most importantly, your child feels understood and thought of, which from an attachment perspective helps her to feel secure, so although you may disappoint her by not fixing or trying to fix her problem, it is okay because you are on her side and she is on your mind.

Reflecting should generally be used when emotions are high and provocations are flying your way. It is invaluable not only for managing difficult emotions but also for helping your children understand their emotions and themselves. You are in the best position to understand your child's emotions, and your child relies on you to help them make sense of their own emotions from birth through to adulthood.

What is sobering is that you and your partner are usually the only ones who will consistently and most powerfully provide reflections to your children.

- Their siblings won't do it. They will at best respond to emotional provocations, but are more likely to react and often quite intensely.
- Their friends won't do it. Just like their siblings, a provocation is almost certainly going to result in a reaction.
- Their teachers may or may not do it. Quite aside from the pressures of running a class of twenty or thirty kids, the teachers generally do not have the strong emotional connection to your child that you do. (Of course, a teacher who is reflective will find their job much easier as their own feeling brain will be less activated, and they will have an emotional teaching role as well as their more usual 'logical/ content' teaching role.)
- Therapists and counsellors will reflect, but that is to be expected as being reflective is a prerequisite skill for effective counselling. But most counsellors will see your child on a weekly or less-frequent basis, and your child's experience of

the therapist's reflections will be easily drowned out if the more important attachment objects in their life (their parents) continue to be reactive. It is for this reason that in my treatment recommendations I usually advise parent work prior to considering individual work with a child. A therapist should never do with a child something that they can teach a parent to do.

COMBINING REFLECTING AND RESPONDING

Though children generally know what our answer or response is going to be, there are times when a specific response is required. In these circumstances, one option is to reflect first, leave some silence, respond and answer the provocation, then finish with reflection.

For example, your child wants to go to an unsupervised party, and is very upset that you won't let them go.

Reflecting: 'You'd really like to go to that party' (short silence).

Responding: 'You can't go honey because there will be no parent there.'

Reflecting: 'But I know you'd really like to go.'

Ben and Nick

Four-year-old Ben has been asking for an ice-cream for ten minutes, ever since the TV was turned off. His father, Nick, is becoming increasingly frustrated at having to say no, and explaining that it will spoil his dinner. Eventually Ben goes to the freezer, opens it and takes out an ice-cream. Some of the ways Nick might react, respond and/or reflect are as follows:

Reacting

- 'I'm sick of this! Just take the ice-cream and get out of my sight!'
- 'Right. I'm not talking to you!' Nick ignores Ben.
- 'You naughty boy!' Nick grabs the ice-cream and puts it back.

- Nick snatches the ice-cream, slams the freezer door and snaps, 'That's it! Go to your room!'
- Nick smacks Ben and shouts 'When will you learn?!'

Responding

- 'You can't have an ice-cream.' Nick calmly returns it to the freezer.
- 'I've told you no. If you don't put it back by the time I count to three you won't have one for dessert, either.'

Reflecting

- *Thoughtful silence:* Nick looks at Ben, trying to understand his motivation. Is he too hungry to wait another few moments for dinner? Does he want attention? Does he want to punish Nick for turning off the TV earlier?
- *General reflection:* 'You really want that ice-cream. It's hard to not get what you want.'
- *Specific reflection, modified:*
    - 'You don't like it when I say no or disagree with what you want.'
    - 'It makes you angry when I don't do what you want. I wonder if you want me to do whatever you say.'
    - 'I wonder if you are still angry at me for turning off the TV.'

Reflecting-responding-reflecting

- 'You really want an ice-cream now don't you? But we're having dinner in a little while so you can't have one just yet. But I know you'd like to have it right now.'
- 'It's hard to not get what you want, whether it's an ice-cream or TV. You can't have the ice-cream Ben. It's hard to miss out sometimes.'

Sarah and Cathy

Ten-year-old Sarah wanted to go to a friend's house after school, but her mother, Cathy, said no because the friend lived in another suburb and she didn't have a car to collect her (it was being repaired). After a few minutes of bargaining Sarah became angry. 'You *never* do anything I want! I hate you! You always let Michelle (sixteen-year-old sister) go wherever she wants to!' Some of the ways Cathy might react, respond and/or reflect are as follows:

Reacting

- 'Oh, just shut-up!'
- 'That's so unfair! I take you everywhere.'
- 'You make me so angry!'
- 'You have no right to be angry at me considering everything I do for you.'
- Cathy walks away and ignores Sarah for the rest of the night.

Responding

- 'You know we don't have a car today.'
- 'It's just not going to happen tonight.'

Reflecting

- *Thoughtful silence:* Cathy watches Sarah, trying to understand her response. Perhaps her friendships at school are under stress and she is feeling left out; perhaps she is feeling envious of her sister.
- *General reflection:*
  - 'I can see you're really upset about this.'
  - 'I can see you're angry at the moment. Anger's okay, Sarah; but screaming at me is not.'
- *Specific reflection, modified:*
  - 'It's really important for you to see your friend this afternoon for some reason. I wonder why.'
  - 'It must seem that I'm not being fair to you and not trying hard enough to help you get what you want.'

Reflecting-responding-reflecting

- 'I know you want to go see your friend tonight. But you can't since we don't have a car to collect you. I can see it's upsetting you to miss out on what you want.'

Jade and Liz

Fourteen-year-old Jade has been refusing to go to school for three months, complaining of stomach pain and headaches. These have been fully investigated and all the adults have a united position that her symptoms are due to anxiety. A plan that Jade has agreed to has been put in place for her to return to school, but on the morning of return Jade complains of her worst headache ever.

Reacting

- Liz says worriedly, 'Oh, honey. That sounds awful. You'd better stay home then.'
- 'I'm sick of you hanging about the house!'
- 'I hope you're not thinking about staying home from school today!'
- 'Do you want to just stay at home and end up being a nothing?'
- 'I can't handle this anymore. I give up. Stay home then – see if I care.'
- 'It's your life. Screw it up if you want!'
- 'Get out of the house *now!*'
- (Liz manhandles Jade into the car) 'You're going and that's it!'

Responding

- 'You agreed that the plan today is to go to school.'
- 'We've been through all this. You need to go to school today.'
- 'Whether you're at home or at school you'll still have a headache, so you may as well be at school.'

Reflecting

- *Thoughtful silence:* Liz wonders what it must be like for Jade; how safe home seems, how hard it may be for her to catch up on missed work, coping with all the comments by friends about where she has been, how fear is a 'mind killer' and she may not be thinking straight.
- *General reflection:*
    - 'It must feel really awful to have a headache.'
    - 'It's really difficult to go to school sometimes.'

- *Specific reflection, modified:*
  - 'I wonder if you think I'm being a bit cruel by making you go to school.'
  - 'I wonder if you are a bit worried about being back at school and what the other kids will say.'
  - 'I know you'd like me to say it's okay to stay home from school. I wonder if you are really worried about what might happen at school today.'

Reflecting-responding-reflecting

- 'I know you have a headache and you'd really like to stay home today. But you have to be brave and go to school, Jade; that was what we agreed in those meetings, even though I know you'd like to stay here.'

The more skilled you can become at recognising, understanding and reflecting your children's emotions, the more skilled your children will become at recognising and managing their own emotions. However, if you find your balance is too heavily weighted towards reactivity (remember, some reactivity is normal and unavoidable), and, despite your best efforts, you find your emotions constantly triggered by your children, this may indicate that you have your own unresolved emotional difficulties.

If this is the case, it is important to seek out your own help, which may include professional mental health assistance, or to deal with any past issues that keep you stuck in unhelpful ways of thinking and interacting. Perhaps you need to take stock of your work–life balance, your relationships and change some priorities. The benefit of entering a therapeutic relationship is that you will experience someone being reflective with you; it is always more powerful to experience something than to read about or be told something.

Your children need you to understand them and to reflect that understanding and acceptance. What better gift could you give them? It won't be easy, and there will be suffering, but at least you and your children will be suffering for a purpose: their development into strong, brave, free, playful, accepting, curious, empathetic and emotionally and relationally capable young adults.

BIBLIOGRAPHY

John Gottman, *Raising an Emotionally Intelligent Child: The Heart of Parenting*, Simon & Schuster, 1997.

Elisabeth Muir, Mirek Lojkasek and Nancy Cohen, *Watch, Wait and Wonder: A manual describing a dyadic infant-led approach to problems in infancy and early childhood*, Hincks-Dellcrest Institute, 1999.

Donald Winnicott, *Playing and Reality*, Routledge Classics, 2005.

Donald Winnicott, *Winnicott on the Child*, De Capo Press, 2005.

ACKNOWLEDGEMENTS

To my wife and children, I thank you for your patience, support and kindness as I worked on this project – it would not have happened without you.

To my parents, I thank you for being wonderful role models as I raised my own children; your wisdom and experience will live on through your grandchildren.

To my colleagues, I thank you for your generosity in sharing your skills and helping me in my professional development these past seventeen years. To all those who read earlier manuscripts, I thank you for your patience and advice.

To my editor, Miriam Cannell, your guidance was invaluable. Your professionalism mixed with optimism and support made finishing this project both possible and enjoyable. Thanks also to Caz Brown for her inspired design work.

And finally, special thanks must go to all the children, adolescents and families with whom I work – your courage and bravery as you strive to create change is the true inspiration for this book.

NOTES